To scott

HOW SNEAKERS RUINED MY LIFE

The Entrepreneurial Journey That Shifted My Mental State

Book 2

How Sneakers Ruined My Life
The Entrepreneurial Journey That Shifted My Mental State

Copyright © 2021 by Exclucity

ISBN 978-1-7775245-1-7

First Edition
Published by:
Exclucity

Printed in Canada by Sure Print & Design

To My Mother –

I know parts of this book will be alarming to you.

No mother wants to read about her son's pain.

I'm sorry.

CONTENTS

SYNOPSIS OF BOOK 1

How Sneakers *Saved* My Life

Welfare, bankruptcy, arrests, failed businesses, and more. In Book 1, *How Sneakers Saved My Life*, Trent rips the covers off and takes us on the roller-coaster ride that is his life.

While some of Trent's life experiences are shocking to read, his journey is captivating and you will find yourself rooting for his success along the way, especially during his most difficult years.

The book starts off with a short story about Trent's grandmother migrating to Canada from Jamaica on a government program that violated her human and civil rights, then he openly tells us of his life as a child growing up in an abusive home. As soon as you feel his pain, Trent keenly shows us that "No one should ever let their circumstance become their excuse." We witness him succeed regardless.

The chapters in Trent's first book uniquely move back and forward between times in his life, keeping you paying attention to each line. He details how he brought Exclucity from the trunk of his car to the national stage, includes a police chase that will have you on the edge of your seat, and introduces the first company he started at just 12 years old. Trent also shares stories about his gambling past, being banned from the USA, modelling in New York City and South Africa, sourcing in China, getting kicked out of high school and only having $3.52 to his name.

Not one page of this autobiography is boring.

If all of that isn't enough for a 200-page book, Trent still finds time to give sneakerheads an insider's look into key moments in 2012 which he believes is the year that changed sneaker culture forever.

If you're a young or eager entrepreneur, you will learn so much from this book, and if you're not, that's fine too, there are enough life lessons in it for someone of any age to learn from.

Trent's life is a MOVIE!

Book 1

Available Now

HOW SNEAKERS SAVED MY LIFE

My Entrepreneurial Journey

An Autobiography By: TRENT

TRENT 1 | GROWING UP IN PAIN

EXCLUCITY 1 | BUILDING A STARTUP

TRENT 2 | YOUNG, DUMB & IGNORANT

EXCLUCITY 2 | BUILDING A BRAND

-FOREWORDS By:

Will Shelby (Former Nike Director)

Nick Nestor (Former Nike Territory Sales Rep)

Re'shaun D. (A "Day One" Exclucity loyalist)

TRENT 3 | 2015

Thinking about ME

2015

Thinking about ME

It was Tuesday, September 8, *2015*, the day after Labour Day, and I had just spent the last three months jumping from one hotel to another. I opened up my first Toronto brick-and-mortar location in July and in the months leading up to it and after I had no permanent place to live. Needless to say, I was stretched thin, feeling out of sorts and exhausted.

Let me start off by saying that I had a lot of help with the launch of my new location! Having an amazing staff took a lot of stress off me, but what most people don't realize is that even if an entrepreneur has 1000 amazing people helping, it only relieves physical stress. While that is amazing, it doesn't always do much for the mental stress of entrepreneurship.

I felt that I've always done a good job when it comes to dealing with my mental stress, but I can remember that I started feeling extremely anxious around the time I opened my fourth location. That increased tenfold when I was opening up my fifth location in Toronto *in 2015*. It was the first in Toronto but fifth overall in Canada.

People say opening up your second location is the hardest part of expanding a business because it is the first time you will ever have to run a store without physically being there. The next difficult transition is when you open a location in another province or state. For me, opening my second location wasn't that bad but opening up in Toronto really stressed me out.

It took a toll on me....

. . .

I truly don't think customers understand all the steps that it takes to open up just one retail location. And I'm not only talking about a sneaker store but any kind of retail operation. It's exhausting.

It takes a minimum of about one year of serious hardcore planning before I can even open the doors, then three to six months after that to fix all the things that I messed up. (There are always mess-ups regardless of how many locations you open.) So, it's basically a two-year process full of stress.

Now, take all of that and add the fact that Ontario was a brand-new province for me; new things to learn, new permits to apply for, new staff to hire, everything was new. I was basically starting from scratch. To make matters worse, I still had four locations that were already open in Montreal and three of them were fairly new.

On top of ALL that, I had extra pressure on me. I couldn't let anything slide while opening any of my new locations because all eyes were on me. Since I was expanding so aggressively, it was like being in a fish bowl and everyone was watching, from suppliers to competitors. Some were rooting for me but most were not. Some assholes were even trying to do shit in the background to stop my momentum.

Not an Easy Road

"From the minute of birth, you enter this earth/ Obstacles deh inna your way to overcome first/" - Buju Banton, Jamaican reggae dancehall recording artist

. . .

One thing that I did not speak about much in Book 1 is that I own 100% of Exclucity. From day one, I've never had a partner or an investor to lean on if and when shit hits the fan. When I sign a multi-million-dollar ten-year lease, it's my name and my name only that is on it. I'm fully liable for every penny.

And it doesn't stop there.

With each lease I sign, of course, comes a new location, which means hydro, telephone, and internet bills that I am responsible for as well, plus a tonne of other services needed to run and operate a storefront location.

Oh yeah, and then there is the responsibility of paying the staff, buildout costs, and inventory. Not to mention hundreds of other things. It never ends.

When major retailers or restaurants like Starbucks open a new location, it's just as hard. The only difference is that they have teams and departments that handle all the phases until projects are completed. They also have a big pile of money to pull from, and if the money runs out, there is a lot more where that came from.

When you're an independent retailer and your parents are immigrants from Jamaica that came to Canada with literally nothing, shit is a bit harder and way more stressful. If I mess up there's no pile of money that will cushion my fall or anyone to hand off things. If I fuck up, I'm packing up my bags and it's a wrap for me. There is no soft place for me to land and I'll be on the streets.

Now, having said all of that, please don't get me wrong even for a second. I wouldn't want it any other way. If we're in the finals and the series is tied 3-3, we're down by two with four seconds left on the clock, GIVE ME THE FUCKING BALL!! I want the last shot, AND I'm taking a three, I'm not looking for the lay-up. That's just how I'm built; I want this life. I put myself in this position for a reason. I don't want to live any other way.

I'm not this way because of the money, not at all. Money is just a point system that lets you know how well you're doing. I actually hate money; to me, it isn't even real. I want this life for the possibilities that it can bring me.

I do this for the chance to take the three-point shot and to see it go in. That's the best feeling in the entire world.

To me, that is living….

. . .

As much as I love this life, I made a huge mistake while working tirelessly for my dreams. I got caught up and forgot about ME.

I was living **for** my dream instead of living my dream.

From October 21, 2012, to July 25, *2015,* I opened stores back-to-back with no breaks in between and I was starting to run on fumes. My mental tank was basically on empty.

Some of you may be saying… "Hey Jackass, why didn't you just take a break?"

Great question, let me answer that.

As I mentioned in Book 1, Nike and other suppliers will support a retailer's vision, but also notice that nowhere in that section did I ever say anything about suppliers holding your hand and babying you through the process either.

I had a window of opportunity to grow in a time when Nike was hot, if it wasn't me, it would have been someone else. Suppliers are not going to sit by and wait for you but will find someone else to do the job. I had an opportunity and I needed to strike while the iron was hot!

. . .

(Now that you're all caught up on my drama, let's go back to the beginning of the book.)

It was September 8, *2015*, the day after Labour Day. I called a meeting with my general manager of stores, Khloe, and brand manager and assistant buyer, Dan, to let them know that I would no longer be working in the stores with the staff on the floor. I was going back to Montreal indefinitely. It was time to start...***Thinking About ME***.

It wasn't an easy decision for me to make but I knew I could trust Khloe and Dan to run the day- to-day operations without me. Khloe had been working at Exclucity since I had my first location. I had personally trained her on the fundamentals for years and she had been essential in our growth thus far.

I left Khloe in charge of operations.

Dan had the same kind of rise within the company; he was there with me from the first store. He knew just as much as I did about sneakers, if not more. Dan was young, knew the culture, and he had amazing customer service skills. He was the kind of kid that everyone liked, just a pure heart.

Although in charge of social media and brand management, Dan still worked in the stores from time to time and customers loved him.

Knowing that I had a solid team in both of them, I knew I could finally take some time for myself. Instead of working from the store and serving clients, I could work from home and slow things down a bit. I'd been training Khloe and Dan every day for the past four years and I knew they would excel and elevate the Exclucity brand.

. . .

Prior to opening up the stores, I used to be in the gym every morning but from 2010-2015 I was just too busy. One of the first things I did on my first week working from home was to get back into the gym. I got a gym membership and every morning I woke up and walked 4km to the gym, worked out and then walked back home.

I lived alone, worked alone, and chilled out alone, and I loved it.

Making up for lost time also meant trying to catch up with some friends that I wasn't able to see in a while. I called up one of my oldest friends who had an 8-month-old daughter that I still hadn't met yet. I made arrangements to meet her for the first time.

It's a good thing I have real friends, friends that will hold me down through whatever and not make me feel like shit for missing things because I have a business to run. That's not to be taken lightly as there are many people who don't have that. My family is the same way; they're very supportive, understanding and hold me accountable.

. . .

Whenever I talk at events or do interviews, I'm always asked the same question. "What advice would you give to someone out there that's trying to make it?" And I always reply with exactly the same thing, "Be ready to sacrifice it all, and by all, I mean everything." And I know most of the people in the audience think they understand what I'm talking about but I know they don't have a clue.

"I got a clothing line, I'm a hustler, I do this and that," they say. "Just watch me. In a few years I'm gonna have a Lambo" is what I often hear from young entrepreneurs when I'm at events. It literally hurts my heart.

The hours, research, studying and relentless dedication that it takes to be a successful entrepreneur is mind-blowing and most young entrepreneurs don't think about that. A regular eight-hour workday is not even close to the time that's needed. A lot of young entrepreneurs think the few hours per day that they spend on their business are going to be enough. They have no idea how wrong they are and have no clue what sacrifice truly is.

I've had several failed businesses before Exclucity was successful. I've failed over and over again, making huge sacrifices along the way just to get back up and try again.

This is what entrepreneurship is truly about.

I drove a light grey minivan with a broken air conditioner when I had my first store. I didn't buy my Range Rover until 13 years after I was in business. And you know what, fuck the material sacrifice, because a lot of people can deal with driving a minivan, but can you deal with your girlfriend or boyfriend being pissed at you for not spending enough time with them? Can you deal with missing birthday parties, concerts, clubbing and vacations? Can you give up your social life and dedicate yourself to your company for 4-5 years till you get it off the ground?

Once you answer that, then think about this.

Will it all be worth it?

Here I was, years later, after all those sacrifices and I was alone in my house calling friends trying to rekindle old relationships, trying to find my way back to having a regular life. I wanted to find the reason why I made the sacrifices in the first place, what were they all for?

I'm very successful. I own a national brand, property, stocks, RRSPs, and I have investments that are well diversified. But guess what I don't have?

I have no life. I have no girlfriend, no wife, and I also don't have any kids.

What's the point of all this? What am I doing all this for? Who will I leave all of this to, my sister's kids? I mean I love them like they are my own but wtf, shouldn't I have my own kids?

This is why I took a break in *2015*. I needed to stop, not only to smell the roses but to also figure out what I was doing all of this for.

I needed to find my purpose and start *thinking about ME.*

EXCLUCITY 3 | 2015
Sidelined by Nike

2015

Sidelined by Nike

I'm a big Oprah Winfrey fan. If you think your favourite rapper is dropping jewels in their raps, trust me, Oprah is the Jay Z, Nas, Mos Def, Queen Latifa, Kendrick or Cordae of TV.

Oprah always gives you something to think about.

"The universe always speaks to us first in light whispers. Then those whispers get louder. Then you get a brick upside your head, and then if you don't pay attention to that, the brick wall falls down (on you)," says Oprah. And then she asks, "Can you catch your whispers before the brick wall comes falling down (on you)?"

That always stood out so much to me.

Every human alive has had a moment in their life when something happens to them and they have said to themselves "hmmm…I have a weird feeling about this." **That's the whisper**!

It's that little weird feeling in your gut. It's so subtle that most of us rarely catch it and we only realize it when it's too late and we say, "Shit, I knew I shouldn't have done that. I should have listened to that feeling."

Thinking back on it now, *2015* was my whisper year, both personally and professionally. I didn't hear the freaking whispers and let me tell you something I got quite a few bricks upside my head. The entire wall almost came all the fucking way down on me, **but** I saved it just before the last brick came down and buried me for good.

I fought back.

Sit back and relax…. I'm gonna tell you how it all went down.

. . .

It was *2015* and my Downtown Toronto store opening was amazing. The Toronto sneaker community came out and embraced us, and all was good. I finally got to do the surprise opening that I wanted to do so many times in Montreal but it never worked out.

I hid the store location from my followers. They all knew we were opening in Toronto but they had no idea where and when. Nineteen hours before opening, I posted this on our Instagram:

"If You're Reading This, It's Not Too Late, We're Opening In 19 Hours"(in the Drake "If You're Reading This It's Too Late" font) and I gave them the address and the restock list.

Everyone went crazy, a massive crowd of people rushed to start lining up within 15 minutes of our post and we were the talk of the city. Exclucity was mentioned on every sneaker blog in Toronto and across Canada, it was great.

Nike was amazed at the buzz I was able to create right out of the gate but on opening day I got my first little Nike whisper.

No one from Nike said anything to me about the store on opening day, but I felt that something was off. A few days later, while we were talking about the opening, someone from Nike asked, "So, are these going to be the tables you're using or are they just temporary?" Then someone else asked, "Are you going to be doing any window displays or just leave it empty?"

It was all subtle comments like that but I got the hint that Nike didn't love my buildout and design of the store. It was the first time they weren't blown away with something that I did.

I didn't make much of it at the time, I just replied, "Yup, these are my tables and, no, I decided to keep the windows clear, this is the store."

Was the store perfect? No, it wasn't but it wasn't much different from any other Exclucity location in Montreal so I didn't see a problem.

About a year and a half before I opened the Downtown Toronto location, the Nike Canada general manager and the vice president of sales brought me to Toronto to tour the city. We were looking to see if I could do in that city what I did with Exclucity in Montreal. The overall goal wasn't to just open one or two Exclucity locations and call it a day. The goal was to open ten to twelve locations in the Greater Toronto Area and the surrounding cities. After that was completed, the next step was to open more locations across Canada.

I would later make the connection as to why Nike had a problem with my buildout and store design, which were attached to my expansion plans. Here's why there was a problem.

. . .

NBA All-Star Weekend in Toronto

My Toronto store that I had just opened didn't look "premium" enough for Nike. The Nike global executives were coming to visit Toronto to make plans for the NBA All-Star Game in a few months and Nike's Canadian leadership team wasn't sure if I had put my best foot forward.

In my channel of the Nike business, everything centres around fashion, street culture, and **basketball**. The upcoming All-Star Game was going to be the first time the game had ever been played outside of the USA, and it was going to be Kobe Bryant's last All-Star Game #RIPKOBE. Also, the GOAT himself, Michael Jordan, was also going to be in attendance.

It was a big moment.

. . .

I've never spent too much money on store buildouts before this, but I think Nike thought I would have stepped up my store design since I was now coming to Toronto and had major expansion plans.

I had opened all five of my Exclucity locations with my own personal money that I had made from selling Long Tees and Durags out the trunk of my car. I didn't have any investors, a trust fund or even a bank loan. I had to watch my money very carefully; I never overspent.

I also couldn't make that Toronto store much nicer than it was because Toronto's rents are crazy. I blew most of my budget on rent. I had to put up three months worth of rent plus a security deposit and the rent was more than double that of any of my Montreal locations.

It wasn't easy to manage but I tried nevertheless.

The NBA All-Star Game was a huge moment in Canadian streetwear culture and I wanted to make sure I had an opportunity to be part of it, even if I wasn't ready for it financially. I wanted to give Exclucity an opportunity to be part of that moment, but I think that move may have caused Nike to *sideline* me.

. . .

One week after my grand opening, just as planned, the Canadian Nike team brought Nike's Global Design team to visit the store to see if they wanted to use it for any of their All-Star installations or product launches for that weekend. I had met a lot of big executives from Nike US before but this team was from GLOBAL -- this was a HUGE deal. This opportunity was the entire reason for making sure I had a store opened in Toronto at this time. I was really excited.

The lead guy on the design team walked into the store, stood at the entrance for about 30 seconds and then said, "Ok, show me upstairs." I brought him upstairs and within a few seconds he remarked, "It's hard to have an activation on the 2nd floor." He walked right back downstairs a few minutes later.

Normally, Nike visits would last 20 to 30 minutes and you talk about the store, get to know each other and ideas start flowing. This visit was nothing close to that and lasted about 5 minutes MAX and then they left.

That was the scariest Nike visit that I ever had but things were about to get much worse for me.

There were more whispers coming.

. . .

On September 1, *2015*, I sent an email to the Canadian vice president of sales at Nike to ask her something about our expansion plans. I was expecting a simple response to my questions, but surprisingly, I got a reply that caught me off guard.

"Let's meet in person to discuss further," her email said.

That's never a good reply to get from anyone. That typically means someone has something bad that they want to break to you but they want to do it in person.

We met a few days later.

The meeting started off slowly with the topic that I already felt was going to be a problem, the Toronto store design. But then weirdly, the conversation was switched to Exclucity's lack of reporting, backend performance, and basically, our overall operations.

I quickly caught on to where this meeting was going.

All of the things I was able to get away with in Montreal when I was on a smaller scale, I was now being told that these things will no longer be accepted. If I wanted to be in Toronto and rival the majors, I had to step up my game and I needed to do them before any more store openings were approved by Nike. By the end of the meeting, it was made crystal clear to me that Exclucity would be *Sidelined by Nike* until these "issues" were resolved.

I left the meeting a bit confused and taken aback, but regardless, I shook hands with the Nike team. I agreed to put a hold on the Exclucity growth strategy until I could come back with a new concept for a store buildout and a revamped backend operation team.

I wasn't upset about what I needed to do because I knew it had to be done at some point. Ultimately, all these changes would benefit Exclucity in the long term. I just wish I could have done it on my terms and not theirs. Most of these issues weren't simple changes that could be done in a few weeks, they were all sweeping changes that would take time and cost a lot of money.

On top of all this, Nike still hadn't told me if they were going to use the store for All-Star Weekend or not. That was still to be decided. The 2nd floor remained empty and not generating any revenue. I hadn't even touched it yet. Nike was dragging their feet and I had to make a move.

Enter Adidas!!!!

. . .

Adidas

In late *2015*, Adidas had hired a great sales rep by the name of Cindy. Cindy was a no-nonsense kind of person, strictly about her business, and I knew she'd be interested in working with me for All-Star Weekend. At the time, Adidas had just dropped the first Yeezy 350 Boost and they were heating up. They were also planning to launch a few new models, Ultra-Boost, NMD and Tubular Doom, which were about to change the game.

Adidas was hungry.

For those of you that are not in the sneaker world, the three models that I just mentioned changed the face of Adidas forever. Thirty years from now, you'll be able to say any of those three models to anyone that's into sneakers and they will know those names.

Two of those new models had a brand-new technology in them called BOOST. Boost is in the Ultra Boost, the NMD and the Yeezy. It would be the first time that any footwear technology would rival "Air," owned by Nike. The debut of those three models shook the entire Nike building for the first time EVER.

Fun fact:

Boost wasn't invented by Adidas. It was licenced by them but it was first offered to Nike. Some sneaker enthusiasts say Nike messed up by not buying/licensing Boost, but I don't agree with them at all. Yes, Boost is super comfortable, and yes, it's a cool technology, but it was Kanye West that made Boost, Boost, not Adidas.

. . .

With Nike on the fence about working with me for All-Star Weekend and Adidas heating up, I emailed Cindy and asked her if she and Adidas would be interested in taking over the 2nd floor for that weekend. We jumped on a call and chatted for 10-15 minutes before she said, "I'll have an official offer for you within the next 48 hours."

The next day, Cindy sent me an email with a bunch of Adidas executives copied and there was an amazing offer attached. I knew from day one that Cindy was about her business but I was blown away!!! Adidas was offering me a full TAKEOVER of the 2nd floor at my Downtown Toronto Queen St. location. They weren't only offering to take it over for All-Star Weekend but to do so for two months!

The offer came complete with an action plan, launch parties, activations, and a tonne of exclusive sneaker releases. The official Canadian launch of the Tubular Doom and NMD would be held at MY STORE exclusively.

That's a mind-blowing offer.

Forget about the money for a second, it was more of an honour to me more than anything. The money was irrelevant at this point. Adidas is a global powerhouse brand. It's crazy to get an offer like that from a brand like Adidas.

But I still didn't accept it right away.

As crazy as the offer was, in my heart I still wanted Nike to do the TAKEOVER and Cindy knew that. Everyone knew that and that's probably why Adidas made the deal so sweet to begin with. I replied quickly to Cindy's offer saying how honoured I was to receive such a great offer but needed some time to think it over because there were other offers on the table and I needed to finish those negotiations first.

. . .

What was taking Nike so long to make a decision? Was it the store design? Was it because it was on the 2nd floor? Could it be because Nike was so busy opening up the Footlocker-owned Jordan store 10 minutes down the street from my store that they didn't have enough time to do anything with Exclucity. I guess I'll never know.

A few weeks after my meeting with Nike, the general manager called to tell me that Nike Global had made a final decision not to do anything on the 2nd floor. I wasn't shocked, I felt that it was going to be a no anyway but I had to hold on to find out.

I immediately called Cindy and accepted Adidas's offer. It's not what I wanted but still nothing to complain about. I had the 2nd biggest sport brand in the world lined up to do two months of activations, parties and sneaker launches at my store.

That's something to be proud of.

. . .

In October *2015*, I was one month into my "work from home" plan. I was supposed to be at home winding down, relaxing and trying to find myself, but as you can see that's not what was really happening. I was working on deals that can be even more time-consuming and definitely more stressful than working in the stores and overseeing day-to-day operations. I was flying back and forth for meetings every week, sometimes a few times a week.

My work-life balance was getting to me.

. . .

Online

I can't talk about Exclucity *2015* without talking about online. I'll touch on it quickly.

Truth be told, back in 2015, I wasn't a big online shopper. I would buy electronics or house supplies but that was really about it. Not being a fan of online shopping was probably the reason why it took me so long to put Exclucity online. It wasn't even my idea to go online; it was one of my sales reps from a smaller sneaker brand that pushed me into it.

One day, he asked me why I wasn't online yet. I told him that my main focus was on opening stores and that I thought footwear would always be an in-store thing since you need to try it on. A size 12 in Converse isn't the same as a size 12 in Nike. And even within Nike, a size 12 Air Max 90 isn't the same as a size 12 Air Force 1.

Clearly, I was wrong. Fortunately, my rep knew that I was wrong and he kept pushing me.

As I began to look more into online, there was one glaring thing that stood out to me -- the possibility of linking all of my stores inventory to one online store. That was a game changer for me. Consolidating my inventory virtually and making it available online were great ways to free up some cash and increase sales. Once I found out I could do that, I was ready to move right away.

One of the main reasons why my Toronto store buildout wasn't over the top was because I didn't have much liquid cash to make subsequent upgrades. Most of my money was tied up in inventory across five separate locations. I had money but it was all in inventory, it wasn't liquid. Online was really going to help me liquefy some of that cash.

Using my own money and being a sole owner was always one of my main priorities. Online helped me hold out from getting a loan or selling a percentage of Exclucity to be more liquid.

It's best to hold out on loans, investors and partners as long as possible. Make your business as profitable and as attractive as possible with your own money then when you're ready to sell a percentage you can ask for more.

. . .

My team, led by Khloe, got online set up in a few months and we got the green light from Nike and the other brands to sell online. I set a goal to launch online on November 21, *2015*, the weekend before Black Friday. Of course, I set up a huge restock to launch the site and as expected it got a lot of attention within the sneaker community but it was also met with resistance.

Prior to Exclucity being online, most of the stores in my category/territory used online as a secondary store. Meaning, these stores would release a shoe Saturday 10am in-store, and if that shoe didn't sell out by Monday morning for example, then they would put the remaining sizes (we call it, a broken size run) online.

Typically, they were the smallest and biggest sizes.

I saw things differently. Although I wasn't a huge online shopper and I was focused on opening brick-and-mortar stores, I still knew that there were people who lived in the middle of nowhere. They didn't have access to most of the hyped releases that we carry and I knew that they wanted access. That's who I was going after, I saw it as an opportunity to build a national following while making money. But like I said, my idea was met with resistance.

After I posted my restock on social media, I got a call from my Nike rep who had some questions. "Hey, are you sure you want to sell all that online, that's a lot of high energy product? Most stores keep that kind of energy for their in-store purchases." I quickly replied, "Yes I know, that's exactly why I'm doing it!"

Being the first to market with something is usually the best option.

Is it risky sometimes? Yes, of course it is, it could blow up in your face, but **"With great risk often comes great reward."**

In the months to follow, most of the stores in my category/territory started to change their approach to online and today this is the industry standard.

. . .

2015 was a hell of a year.

I got my first Toronto location open, I launched my first online store, and I had negotiated a deal with Adidas to open a two-month activation pop-up store that would launch All-Star Weekend.

I didn't get the rest I needed in 2015 but I was grateful for the blessings that I had.

I finished out the year working hard and I planned to get the rest I needed in 2016, which did not happen.

There is always something! ALWAYS!

TRENT 4 | 2016

The Mansion

2016

The Mansion

Knowing that I wasn't going to be opening any new stores in *2016* because of Nike's decision to sideline me, I figured maybe it was time to treat myself to something nice. While I was pissed at Nike's decision, I was low-key happy that I could finally get a break.

Over the past four years, I had opened a new store every year and I equated opening new stores to winning a championship because of all the long hours of hard work. I had just gone back-to- back to back-**to-back.** Jordan didn't even do that, lol. It was time to celebrate.

. . .

What qualifications need to be met for a house to be called a mansion?

Realtor.com:

"Technically, realtors term mansions as houses that have at least 8,000 square feet of floor space."

Merriam-Webster's dictionary:

"simply stating that a mansion is "a large and impressive house: the large house of a wealthy person."

<u>Zillow.com:</u>

A mansion is a very large house; somewhere between 5,000 and 8,000 square feet. ... A mansion is also defined by luxury: tennis courts, large open foyers, grand staircases, crystal chandeliers.

Are you confused?

Good, cause so am I and to be honest with you I don't give a fuck what Webster, Danny, or Kevin have to say. Lol!

My house has six bathrooms, a princess staircase, more than 20 rooms and I have 3 chandeliers. My bedroom has couches, a huge TV, a bar cart, and a two-way fireplace connected to the bathroom.

Bitch, I live in a damn mansion, ok.

And just in case my house doesn't technically fit into the definition of what a mansion is, I named my house THE MANSION, now nobody can say shit. Lol!

. . .

The whole "mansion" nickname started out as an inside joke between a good friend and me, and has now turned into a popular joke amongst my family and friends. Everyone is in on the joke now. Whenever my friend would call me while I was house hunting, I'd answer my phone and say, "Hey, I'm busy looking at mansions right now, can I call you back?" LOL! Then my realtor got in on the joke as well and he would call me and say, "Hey Trent, what's up? You ready to go look at mansions." It's really funny.

I can get away with making these kinds of jokes with my family and friends because they know it was really just a joke and nobody takes it seriously. They all knew I was excited and proud to be in the position to be able to be looking at these kinds of homes. I was elated and wanted to share that with the people closest to me.

My father grew up in a one-bedroom house in Jamaica that accommodated more than ten people. My mother also grew up in Jamaica and she lived in the countryside with no electricity and had to use an outhouse. Knowing where my parents came from, could you blame me for being so happy and proud of myself for fulfilling the promise I made to my mother when I was five or six years old?

Most little kids grew up wanting to be a doctor, a firefighter or a veterinarian, something conventional like that. When I was five or six years old, I told my mom that I was going to be a businessman, would buy her a Jaguar, and planned to live in a mansion.

If you read Book 1, you'll know the first thing I did when I started making good money was to buy my mother a brand-new Mercedes Benz. I drove it up to her house with a big ass red bow and everything. Knowing that I had "buying my mom a car" checked off my bucket list, I knew that my next goal was to invest in the house of my dreams -- a mansion!

For many years prior to this, I was nervous about buying anything too expensive because owning a business is so volatile and you never know when you'll need cash. A few slow months and things could turn bad quickly. One of the things that made me feel better about buying a big home was that at the end of the day it's real estate. If I buy smart, it's an investment and something that I can leave for my kids and their kids. Mansions or big houses, whatever you want to call them, can be extremely profitable in the long term. I looked at it as a business and bought accordingly.

As excited as I was, I was also very nervous. Just like the store(s), all the responsibilities and extras were on me alone but I promised myself to have fun with it and to enjoy the moment. After all, this was the whole point to everything I was doing with my business.

Building generational wealth.

. . .

After a few months of looking at a number of homes and narrowing it down to just two choices, I decided to involve my family in the process.

I brought my entire family with me to help me pick which house to buy.

I knew going back for a second visit with a bunch of people oohing and ahhing about the house would most likely hurt me in the negotiations but I had to do it anyways. This was a moment for my family to enjoy and I couldn't pass it up. My mom and my sister's kids made me the most nervous because I knew they wouldn't be able to hold back their excitement. There was no way I'd be able to act like I wasn't interested in the house during negotiations afterwards, but like I said, I had to do it.

It's not just my house; it's our house.

My realtor set up both appointments on the same day and we showed up to the first house together. It was my mom, my dad, my sister, her husband and their four kids, ages 4, 8, 10, 12, **and** my aunt on my mother's side.

That's a total of ten people including me. There was no possible way that my plan of trying to keep everybody chill was going to work but I tried anyways.

As we walked in the door, everyone was quiet, cool, calm and collected. My sister was trying her best to keep the 4-year-old calm and my bother-in-law was the same with the 8 year old, even though they were told beforehand to keep quiet. We all knew it wasn't going to be an easy task.

The couple that was living there came to greet us and said they would step out and give us the freedom to look around and talk. As soon as the couple started to walk away the two younger kids began yelling and freaking out. They didn't even wait five seconds to let the couple get out the door. I looked over to see what my mom was doing and yup, I knew it, she was in the middle of her ugly cry.

I looked back to see if the couple had made it out the door but they were just at the door putting on their shoes and they saw everything. Negotiations out the window... lol!

The kids ran around the house like they were at one of those massive indoor playgrounds with nets, swings, and nerf balls. My sister went after them and I walked over to my mom to console her. "I just wish your grandmother was alive to see all of this," she said.

My grandmother, Ethlyn Harris, who I speak about at length in Book 1 -- the lady who I try to model myself after and the matriarch of our family -- had passed away a few months ago and it was weighing on our hearts heavily.

I hugged my mother and told her that I was alone with my grandmother in the hospital a few days before she passed and had shown her some pictures of the homes I was thinking of buying. I told her that it was okay and that she didn't have to cry because grandma knew about my plans.

My grandmother will never be able see or hold any of my children, nor will she ever see me get married. My house and my business are all I had to show her. I know a house, money or material things don't equate but I got some comfort in knowing that she died knowing her grandson was a success.

My grandmother was the reason that all of us are here in Canada. It was because of her sacrifice and her selflessness that I was even able to buy a home or start a business in this country. She came to Canada as a maid in the 60s and slept in a closet so that I could have an opportunity to be great. I had to let her know that her struggles were not in vain.

Of course, all of this made my mother cry even more, but the couple had left at this point so it was all good.

We spent about two hours looking at the first house and then went to see the second one, which we unanimously selected. Well, almost all of us. My little nephew liked "his room" better in the first house, but when I told him that I planned to redesign the entire house and would make "his room" how he wanted it, I got his vote.

. . .

I spent the next few months having buyer's remorse and literally freaking out over the house that I bought. I remember the first night I was alone in it walking around and thinking that I just made the biggest mistake ever. I thought about selling it right away and to just take my losses. It was really overwhelming.

I think that's a typical thing most entrepreneurs go through. When is it time to spend some of your earnings on yourself? You spend most of your time thinking about your company and what it needs, always making sure it has the finances that it needs to grow while it goes through its ups and downs.

I thought I chose the best time to buy a house because I had been profitable for so many years. I had saved up and planned to buy a home for a few years before committing to actually doing it. I ran over every scenario with my financial team and it was the right time. The house was the right price and everything looked great. But in business, nothing is ever certain and it turned out to be the worse time ever.

My house just ended up adding to my stress as I started to have financial issues in the following years to come.

At the time I purchased my house, I had no idea how bad my money issues were about to get. I had heard a few whispers and my gut was telling me something but I pressed on.

I wish that I had just listened to those whispers.

EXCLUCITY 4 | 2016
ADIDAS & YEZZY

2016
ADIDAS & YEZZY

Ok, let's go!

Let's get into my roller-coaster ride with Adidas that ended with me making an impactful decision that caused ripples across the Canadian sneaker industry. I'm going to cheat a little bit in this section and tell you about Adidas from *2016* to 2018. It's better to get the story all in one shot. What a fucking nightmare…

Here's what happened.

. . .

Before I start my story, I'm going to give the readers who are not "sneaker enthusiasts" a quick recap of Adidas's monumental accomplishment and how they put the entire Nike building in shock.

In 2015, Adidas made a big splash when they signed Kanye West and released the first Adidas YEZZY Boost 750. After that, they made some noise with the launch of the Tubular Doom with Ronnie Fieg at New York Fashion Week and continued that same energy with Kanye when he wore the triple white Adidas Ultra Boost on stage at one of his concerts.

When Kanye West left Nike for Adidas nobody thought Adidas or Kanye would ever be able to affect Nike. Since the late 80s, Nike has always been the dominant leader in the sneaker space and nobody has ever even come close to knocking them off.

Until *2016*...

Adidas was hot and they were ready to take it up a notch in *2016* by bringing more YEZZYs and introducing Tubular Doom, NMD, and Ultra Boost to the mass market. The goal was to put a thorn in Nike's side for the first time in over two to three decades and to create an entire new movement based in Boost.

. . .

Pop-Up Shop

Here's a post from my Instagram account Feb. 9, *2016* Instagram:

"The Takeover"

As I sit down on my couch looking at 3D drawings for a store that I'm about to launch with Adidas, my mind wonders off and I start thinking back to when I was a kid.

Never in my wildest dreams could I ever have imagined that one day I'd be involved in building and opening up a retail store with one of the most iconic brands in the entire world. Of course, we all have big dreams as kids but do we actually think they will ever happen? How could I be launching a store with the same brand that worked with one of the most important groups in music history? Salute to Kanye West and all but it was Run DMC that made me want to rock "MY ADIDAS."

I often blog about waking up early, working hard, setting HUGE goals, loving your HATERS, staying focused, keeping your family close and most importantly, living your truth. Today, I present you proof that everything above really does happen when you set your mind to it.

It's with great honour and humbling pride that I announce to you that EXCLUCITY will be partnering up with the iconic Germany-based brand, better known as Adidas, for a first of its kind "launch" store and it will be located on the 2nd floor of the EXCLUCITY location at 552 Queen St. W., Toronto, Ontario.

Thanks to everyone who has played a part in making this happen. It's going to be an amazing ride.

Stay tuned for opening information.

(Note: Montreal, we haven't forgotten about you. More info coming soon!!)

"Walk with me. I got something to say"

T

No one at Adidas asked me to do that. The post was just me genuinely speaking from the heart.

Adidas is an ICONIC brand, arguably more iconic than Nike in some people's eyes, not mine but someone could make a legit argument.

The iconic RUN DMC was the first Hip Hop group in history to sign an endorsement deal with a sneaker brand and it was with Adidas. In the 80s, dance crews weren't breakdancing in Air Maxs, they were wearing and breaking in Adidas and Puma. Adidas owned cool in the early to mid 80s and it wasn't till Nike signed Michael Jordan in 1984 that things started to shift.

Quick Fun Fact:

Michael Jordan wasn't happy with his second signature shoe, the Air Jordan 2, and he was thinking about leaving Nike for Adidas. Nike heard about the rumours and quickly called Michael and teamed him up with an up-and-coming designer named Tinker Hatfield. They worked on the Air Jordan 3 together and Michael was so happy with it (to date, Michael Jordan's favourite shoe) that he decided to stay.

Tinker and Michael went on to design the most popular signature footwear line in the history of sneakers -- something that will probably never happen again. Had Michael left Nike and gone to Adidas things would have been completely different in the world of sneakers.

. . .

Now that you know the love I have for Adidas as a brand, here is what Adidas thinks of Exclucity.

This is article that came out in Feb 11th *2016*:

MARKETING

BRANDS   ADVERTISING   CONSUMER   MEDIA   TECH   PR   SUBSCRIBE

ADIDAS KICKS OFF ALL-STAR WEEKEND WITH A POP-UP SHOP

The global sportswear brand has opened a Toronto sneaker boutique

REBECCA HARRIS | FEBRUARY 11, 2016

Adidas is stepping into the pop-up space with a second floor takeover of Toronto sneaker boutique, Exclucity.

The Adidas shop will give customers access to exclusive Adidas Originals launches and will act as a reveal space for new products in the coming months. This month, the Adidas shop will be dedicated to the new Tubular line of sneakers, as well as official NBA All-Star apparel and footwear.

The space itself features Adidas branding, custom imagery by Toronto photographer Horace Ng, a 3D map of Toronto and customer photo activations.

MARKETING

BRANDS ADVERTISING CONSUMER MEDIA TECH PR SUBSCRIBE

Exclucity was founded in Montreal, where it has three locations and another in Laval. It opened its first Toronto location on Queen Street West last fall.

"Exclucity has got amazing credibility in the sneaker culture, and lifestyle and music world," said **Melanie Cammalleri**, category brand planner at Adidas Canada. "For us, it was just a great opportunity to partner with a brand like that, especially during an exciting time around NBA All-Star Weekend in Toronto."

The shop was initially going to be open for a couple of months, but it may be open longer. "Everybody who is involved in it is really happy with how it turned out, so as of right now, it's sort of indefinite," said **Renzo Mendoza**, trade marketing manager at Adidas Canada.

"The ability to tell our brand story with a partner like Exclucity, in the location that it provided, and with an already established consumer base is phenomenal," added Mendoza.

To market the shop, Adidas Canada will use the brand's new global hashtag, #MyFuturels, which focuses on monthly product launches and monthly stories. It's also doing public relations, blogger outreach and influencer marketing.

"It's more of a grassroots approach. It's getting that natural behaviour of people sharing something with their community," said Cammalleri.

Wow. Reading that again, no joke, gets me emotional.

"Exclucity has got amazing credibility in the sneaker culture, and lifestyle and music world."

"For us, it was just a great opportunity to partner with a brand like that…"

"The ability to tell our brand story with a partner like Exclucity, in the location that it provided, and with an already established consumer base is phenomenal."

Sorry to have to highlight those three lines. I'm sure you caught them in the article but I'm just a little punk ass kid from the West Island in Montreal. I got kicked out of high school and so many people told me I wasn't ever going to amount to anything. It's amazing when I read things like that about a brand that I started from the trunk of my car in Montreal, Quebec. It's still amazing to me.

As you can see, Adidas and I had a great mutual relationship at the beginning of 2016, but that was about to take a turn as we worked together on our store.

. . .

The people I was used to working with at Nike didn't get hired to work there solely because of their ability to crunch numbers. They were hired because they were part of and understood the culture. In my humble opinion, this is where Adidas and Nike differ. Does Adidas have authentic streetwear employees? Of course, they do, though not as many as Nike does and they are just different. I can't quite put it into words but it's just a different environment.

Working side by side with Adidas in *2016* on our store wasn't a great experience for me at all.

From day one, I knew one of the reasons Adidas was partnering up with me was to steal some thunder away from Nike. I was one of Nike's darling accounts and since Nike passed on using my 2nd floor, Adidas took advantage. That's business, I get it and I actually admire it. What I didn't admire was the lack of tact and warmth that Adidas showed the Exclucity staff and me.

My staff, in particular, worked tirelessly over two months to help bring all the events together for Adidas. We had a great All-Star Weekend, everything sold out in seconds and the same happened for the NMD launch. Adidas held huge parties at our store, invited 100s of influencers and brought in DJs form New York. All of the influencers that attended the party got a free pair of NMDs, drinks, food, but Adidas never offered the Exclucity staff much of anything.

It really upset me.

Not only did my staff and I get treated like second-class citizens in our own store/event, but to make matters worse, Adidas didn't follow through with the original deal -- the deal that Cindy sent me and that was so amazing. Not everything in that deal was met.

. . .

The Deal

The deal was that I wouldn't charge Adidas rent and I'd provide and pay the staff but, in return, I would get access to more Adidas product. That never happened, even though it was in writing and approved. I only got a small fraction of what they had promised me, because Adidas had no more product left.

Adidas may have been red-hot, but they had no idea how to manage supply and demand.

Everything that we sold in that pop-up shop was product that Dan and I booked prior to even knowing we were going to be launching a store with Adidas.

Basically, I was funding and staffing the Adidas launch store for them at my own expense.

While I was happy for the opportunity and all the attention this was bringing to Exclucity, a deal is a fucking deal! Adidas isn't a start-up brand struggling to make ends meet; they are a multi-billion-dollar company. They could have done something to fix the situation.

When I took my concerns to Adidas management, all they kept saying was that they were way over budget and had no more money left to do anything to fix the situation at the time.

Even though I was extremely pissed off about all of this, I decided to keep my mouth shut at the time and play the long game. I knew that if Adidas didn't have the money or extra product now, they would be able to take care of me later in the upcoming seasons.

I didn't say anything more about it. I just waited to see how this inventory issue was going to affect the pop-up store. If I didn't have any more Adidas inventory and Adidas didn't have more either wtf was going to happen with the store?

. . .

Shut The Store Down

Unfortunately, as a result of poor planning on the Adidas side of things, The Adidas x Exclucity Launch Store had to shut down abruptly. This was not due to lack of sales or because it wasn't doing well. We had to close it down 30 days after opening because there was no inventory and the store was empty.

I have no idea how something like that even happens, but as I said earlier, Adidas just operates differently. They are new to the world of supply and demand sneaker culture. I don't think Adidas knew how to navigate through it.

But that wasn't the only issue that was on the horizon.

After I got the call that Adidas had decided to close down the store, Adidas brought in a team (that looked more like a wrecking crew) and literally tore the place apart in about half a day. It took Adidas about two to three months to build that store but it took them about five hours to take it all down. They didn't disassemble things but just tore things down. They didn't unscrew things; they ripped them down.

It was a complete nightmare.

When Khloe sent me pictures of how the place looked, I literally jumped on a plane within the hour and went straight to the Adidas head office.

It took me five minutes to find out who was responsible for the damage and I escalated it to senior management and then to the directors. I demanded that a construction crew return to the store and restore it to how it was before they started construction. I had taken pics and videos of the entire place prior to construction, plus it was in our contract that they would return the store to us as it was before they started construction. This would be the second breach of contract since we started. What a fucking nightmare.

I was ready to go to court.

To make a long story short, after a few weeks of back and forth and lawyer's letters, Adidas wrote me a large cheque to repair and restore the entire second floor.

That cheque didn't do anything for me personally, I was still pissed off by what had happened. Adidas couldn't have paid me enough to go through that stress.

But let's forget about the closing of the pop-up shop for now and talk about Adidas as a brand and how their hot streak got superhot, but then cooled down rather quickly.

We had to close the pop-up shop on the second floor because we had no Adidas inventory left. Everything was sold out, but not too long after that – BOOM! -- we had a huge overflow of Adidas inventory and couldn't sell anything unless it had the name YEEZY on it.

It was mind-blowing. It was the first time I'd ever seen a brand die that quickly in my life.

My Adidas issues went from worse to much worse, real quick. We went from no inventory, to wrecking crews, lawyers, too much inventory, and then to me owing Adidas over a million dollars.

"Someone please come get me out of this nightmare."

. . .

Being Late on My Adidas Payments

The Adidas hype was over, and I mean OVER.

After a few months of selling out every release, Tubular came to a screeching halt and completely died and then NMD started slowing down also. Luckily, Ultra-Boost was still doing ok and what was really helping Adidas save face was YEEZY.

YEEZY was still selling out in seconds, every colour, every release but here's the problem with that equation.

Tubular was free to buy in whatever quantities I wanted (no allocations), NMD was allocated to me with fairly big quantities BUT... Ultra-Boost was allocated in small quantities and then YEEZY was allocated in the smallest amount of all four styles.

I had 1000s of pairs of Tubular and Boost product in my inventory that clients no longer wanted to buy and the sales from the limited amount of YEEZYs that Adidas gave me couldn't offset that.

Basically, I owed and was late in paying Adidas close to $1 million because I couldn't sell any Adidas product other than YEEZY.

To add to the situation, I also had another half a million dollars' worth of Adidas product on order that was about to be delivered to the stores and wasn't going to sell either. It was all product that I just saw on liquidation in Europe that I knew I was going to get stuck with because it wasn't going to sell. So, basically, I was in debt to Adidas for close to $1.5 million.

. . .

When I was in Paris for Men's Fashion Week, I noticed that Boost had totally died out in Europe. Every sneaker boutique that I went into in Paris had Adidas on sale. Not only did they have it on sale, but they also had the shoe boxes out on the floor with those big red signs all over them that said LIQUIDATION.

This wasn't just a local issue; it was GLOBAL one.

Boxes on the floor like that and sales signs all over the place? How could Adidas let that happen, ESPECIALLY DURING FASHION WEEK? Nike would have cleaned up the marketplace before ever allowing that to happen. Are you kidding me? That was a huge mistake on Adidas's part.

Adidas had adopted the supply and demand strategy that Nike had popularized and had been doing for years -- make less of the stuff that the clients really want to increase the hype, HOWEVER, Nike basically built the sneaker supply and demand blueprint and as a result Nike knows how to manage their way through the ups and downs in the market. Adidas had no idea how to do that.

And as a result, I GOT FUCKED!

This was the first time that I'd ever been in such debt with a brand. I had no real solution how to fix it, so I thought the best course of action would be to reach out to Adidas and see what we could work out.

. . .

I got on the phone and explained everything to my new sales rep (Cindy, the previous rep had gotten a promotion). I asked him if he could help me out by letting me return some of my Adidas inventory and allow me to cancel some of my orders that were about to be shipped to the stores.

To my surprise, Adidas management pushed back right away and said no.

In my opinion, it was simple. I had a million dollars worth of Adidas inventory and I owed Adidas a million dollars. I was simply asking if I could pay some of my invoices with product.

It wasn't a perfect solution, but it was a solution that could have helped both of us out. It's their product to begin with, they could sell it 10x easier than I could have, and it wouldn't have disrupted the marketplace.

The Adidas leadership team shut my offer down quickly and was only willing to offer me 20K in returns and some markdown dollars, to help me out.

Yes, you read that correctly, that's not a typo. That was Adidas's solution to my $1.5 million issue.

A 20K solution for a $1.5 million problem... Like, wtf.

PLEASE don't get me wrong. I knew that I had to absorb some of the blame here; I was the one who had gotten myself into this mess. I placed those orders, no one else. BUT come on man, $20,000 is all you can come up with? Really?

That wasn't the kind of solution that I was looking for.

My back was up against a wall, I had to make a move. I had to help myself.

. . .

Causing Ripples

The first thing I had to do was stop the bleeding. I had to stop any new Adidas shipment from coming in. That move alone would free me of half a million in debts, but it would of course come at a cost.

I knew that by cancelling all my future orders, Adidas would be pissed off. They would penalize me by removing all my YEEZY allocations but here's what most people don't understand about high-energy/hype products.

That's not where the fucking money is; those releases are all just for clout.

Hype solidifies your store/brand but **you don't make real money off of product that you can't order in mass amounts. Mass product equals mass revenue.** Walmart isn't trendy or cool but check out how much that family is worth. They deal in mass products to mass customers.

In my opinion, the Adidas brand was a high-speed train heading for a cement wall and I needed to get off it before it was too late. Knowing this, I came up with my own plan to get out of Boost, clean up my Adidas inventory, and pay off my debt.

. . .

I set up another call with my new rep and his boss and told them my plan. Since Adidas didn't offer me any relief or aid, I told them I was stuck and had to come up with a plan of my own.

After looking at what I owed Adidas and the Adidas inventory that I had on hand, my only solution was to liquidate my entire Adidas inventory at below cost. That's basically what was happening over in Europe, I wasn't reinventing the wheel, it just hadn't come over here yet.

It was the best solution to help those Adidas invoices that were piling up nonstop.

On the call, my rep and his boss didn't seem too bothered but I think they thought I was bluffing. I have no idea why they would think that but it's the only thing that could have explained why they both called me back the day I started the sale.

They called me in shock as if I didn't tell them exactly what I was doing. They said they knew I was going to have a sale but didn't realize that I was going to put every single Adidas product that I had in inventory on sale.

Let me tell you something. When you owe a million dollars, you do what you've got to do to pay your debts. The entire inventory had to go. ALL OF IT!

. . .

For the whole month, I flooded my social media platforms with the Adidas sale and I disrupted that entire fucking marketplace.

I have friends that work at Adidas, and they told me that their customer service department was flooded with calls about my sale. Clients were calling to see if the Adidas stores were having the same sale as I was, and other retailers were calling in and complaining saying my sale was too big.

I warned Adidas, I told them that this was going to happen, but they didn't want to listen to me.

Upper management was pissed off, but that didn't stop me. I kept pushing my sale. I needed to liquate my inventory.

It's not like Adidas was calling me and saying "Ok, let's try to work something out". That was off the table for them. But they didn't call me because they had a plan of their own.

Instead of helping or trying to make a deal with me, all the Adidas upper management got together and allegedly concocted a story and found a way to spin the entire thing in their favour….

I think they went too fucking far.

Blow Back

I heard rumours that the president, CFO and vice president of sales at Adidas Canada called an emergency meeting and decided to spin what really happened so things wouldn't look so bad on them. They knew a lot of their other retailers were having a hard time selling Adidas also, so they tried to get ahead of it to scare other stores away from matching MY sales.

During this meeting, they allegedly told all the other stores that I was having money issues and that's why I was having this sale. It was also allegedly said that Adidas had decided to cut me out of all Boost and YEEZY products as punishment for Exclucity having this massive 70% off sale. And if any other retailer followed suit with a mass liquidation, the same thing would happen to them.

I understand what Adidas was trying to do. They needed to protect their brand, like I was trying to protect mine, but what I don't think they realized was just how dangerous their move was.

They are a billion-dollar brand, whereas I'm an independent retailer. It's not as easy for me to bounce back from rumours like that. **I chose to get out of YEEZY and Boost** because the dollars didn't add up; it was not their decision.

I made that decision because I knew where the Adidas brand was heading. I thought it was horrible of them to have dragged my business name through the mud like that, just to try and save their own ass.

Where was all the love for Exclucity that Adidas spoke about in the article? What about the credibility we had and the partnership? None of that mattered anymore to them when it came down to the dollars.

It was no longer about the culture and the partnership. It was solely about them.

. . .

Moving on Without Adidas

I felt that Adidas should have done more to help me out but even without their help I still managed to pay off my debt completely. I paid back every penny I owed them.

Months later, around the same time that I finally managed to pay off my debt with Adidas, Adidas Canada brought in an entirely new upper management team that called me into their head office to meet with them to see if we could mend our relationship. They were impressed that I was able to pay off my debt and wanted to make things right and start a new chapter.

I placed a small order with them but since then I haven't bought much Adidas product. Kick me once, shame on you; kick me twice, shame on me.

. . .

Closing the Adidas Pop-Up Shop was difficult, battling back and forth over inventory and invoices was strenuous, but what the Canadian Adidas management team did was really hard on me. They were, allegedly, attempting to discredit my brand and me as a leader, which was fucking hard to deal with. That shit really scared me.

A bunch of other brands started calling me and asking questions. I didn't need that in my life at the time.

I'm no stranger to back-and-forth negotiations, managing a business, and dealing with brands. I actually love it, it gets my juices flowing but the weight of everything was piling up on me so fast during a time when I desperately needed a break.

Years ago, I don't think it would have bothered me as much, but back then I didn't feel all this weight on my back. Things were different now.

TRENT 5 | 2017
Poly-am-o-rous

2017

Poly-am-o-rous

In 2015 and 2016, I tried to make more time for myself but that didn't work out so well. I spent both of those years outside of the actual store trying to manage the company with less of a hands-on approach. But I ended up working harder and increased my stress levels. I was determined to finally start living my life and enjoying the fruits of my labour in *2017*.

It's so crazy to think that I had to push myself and carve out time just to enjoy life but it's a common issue for most successful entrepreneurs, athletes and entertainers. Entertainment and entrepreneurship are very similar in the sense that you're always being pulled in a million different directions. This leads to us giving more time to our craft and the people we employ than to ourselves. When you have staff and people around you that depend on you it's a lot of added pressure. If you slip up and make a mistake, you're not just affecting yourself but the others around you as well. It's a stressful position to be in.

When most of us were kids we looked at the life of a pop star or a powerful CEO and we wished to one day live that life. We want a big house, fancy cars, money, traveling, etc., but what we don't see is the time, hard work and stress that it takes to get into these positions.

Having been in both the music industry and the corporate world, I can say without a doubt they are similar but there is one glaring difference. Pop stars have a much better party life, MUCH BETTER!

In Book 1, I spoke about my music career and going on tour with my artist. I knew the party life very well and, in *2017*, I forced myself to try and get back into it and have some fun again.

Even though I had bought a house in 2016, I couldn't even move in and enjoy it right away because I was working too damn much. I stayed in Toronto working from January till around April *2017*, only flying back to Montreal when needed. It wasn't until late April or early May *2017* that things finally started to calm down at work and I decided it was time to move into my new house and to try to enjoy myself.

Having no free time for myself also meant no time for dating either. I hadn't dated anyone seriously for the past couple of years and I thought that if I made time to get out more and started dating it would help me.

. . .

Poly-am-o-rous: Characterized by or involved in the practice of engaging in multiple romantic (and typically sexual) relationships, with the consent of all the people involved.

"Polyamorous emphasize love and honesty in their multi-partner relationships."

(Oxford Dictionary)

Sa-pi-o-sex-u-al: One who finds the contents of someone else's mind to be their most attractive attribute, above and before their physical characteristics.

For many, defining oneself as Sapiosexual is also a statement against the current status quo of hookup culture and superficiality, where looks are prized above all else. "Give me a deep conversation or a passionate debate over brainless beauty any day."

(Urban Dictionary)

. . .

Throughout my entire life, I've always been very open and honest with women -- very transparent.

I've been in four long-term relationships in my life and I've been engaged twice. If I'm in a relationship with someone, I'm loyal and with them only. But when I'm single and dating, I'm SINGLE, SINGLE!

I grew up in a household where my father constantly lied to my mother about other women. He had multiple relationships with other women while he was married to my mother (actually before and during their marriage) and I saw what it did to her and their relationship. I never want to be that guy.

I think one of the worst things a husband can do to his wife is to have another relationship and lie about it, or vice versa. I can understand meeting someone else and falling out of love and breaking up, that's totally normal. I can even understand making a mistake, coming clean and admitting it. But having a side relationship where you are talking on the phone daily, dating and being there for each other and lying about it. Nah man, that's a YOU problem; you've got something wrong inside you. You're just selfish and lacking consideration for other humans.

I'm not about that life at all.

Another thing that I hate is when men try to lie and play women. They try to pick up women by lying to them and telling them what they think a woman wants to hear, just to try to get them in bed. That is the stupidest thing in the world to me. In my experience, women are attracted to energies, not the stupid shit that comes out of your mouth. I think that most women make 99.9% of their sexual decision based on vibes. Women have the most amazing intuition. Lying to a woman is the single best way to get shut down. It's the worst approach possible. I'm always honest from day one and women appreciate it so much. It makes our connection that much stronger.

My favourite part about being intimate with a woman isn't the technical part of it. What I love the most is the escape, that special place you both go to when things are connecting properly. It's almost like we're levitating together, we're off someplace else and it's just the two of us. It's amazing.

That is what I was missing in my life, that escape. I just may have gone a bit overboard with it when I found it again.

. . .

Dating

Back in *2017*, I was overworked. Going out on dates and partying were the only times I felt totally disconnected from the world. That's not healthy and clearly there was something deeper that was bothering me, but dating and escaping became my drug of choice.

I had no idea that it was just contributing to my pain and ultimately made things worse, but I felt like it was all I had at the time.

I started going out for dinners or drinks almost nightly. I wanted to escape and I was very open about it with everyone who I was dating. I didn't give each woman full details or each other's names but they all knew what I was doing and they were ok with it, especially a woman who I met in Montreal, by the name of Tonya. Oh boy, she was different and wouldn't be upset if I was with other women. Instead, she'd be mad that she missed out and wasn't there with me when I was with another woman.

. . .

When I first met Tonya in 2016, she was always down to hang out and hook up whenever I was in town, but the only problem was that I never really had the time to hang out with her back then. I'd usually text her when I was landing in Montreal and let her know when I was free. I'd go over to her place late at night where we'd have a few drinks, dive deep into some sort of conversation and things would go on from there, then I'd leave in the morning.

We connected quickly and always had a great time. Intimacy is always better when you have a connection with someone and we had a strong connection.

The amazing thing about Tonya is that she was very understanding of my situation. She knew I worked a lot, went back and forth between Toronto and Montreal and that I wasn't looking for anything serious at the moment.

When I first met Tonya, she liked hanging out with me but she was more of a straight-up party kind of woman. She would actually encourage the wildness and always wanted to take things to the next level. There were times when Tonya would invite another woman over to her place to hang out with us. Although I would prefer to be with one woman at a time, being with two women isn't anything to complain about, I guess.

I still made it a point to get to know and have a connection with any woman that came over. We'd have a group text chat and everything; it was fun.

It was *2017*, I was at a place in my life where I was looking to party and Tonya was the perfect one for me at that time.

. . .

On the nights that I was out partying, I'd always be checking my phone, taking calls, and looking at my emails and the stores' Instagram. I was back in Montreal for the summer after having an exhausting first half of the year but I still wasn't getting the total unplugging that I needed.

I needed a vacation.

I knew if I stayed in Montreal, I'd do the same thing that I did in 2015 and 2016. I'd end up overworking myself with some new project and the cycle would continue. If I really wanted to get away from work, I'd have to leave the country for a vacation. I had been working for myself for close to sixteen years and had never taken one, didn't even consider it an option but I knew the time was now. I needed it.

In September *2017*, I gave my sister my cellphone, laptop and keys to the store and took off to Hedonism in Negril, Jamaica. Hedonism is the biggest nudist and swingers' resort in the world. And guess who came with me? The biggest party animal of them all, TONYA!

I gave my sister Tonya's number in case of an emergency and asked her to check my email and cellphone for any urgent calls or messages. I put my email on auto-reply for the first time ever in my life and boarded my flight.

I remember feeling guilty, like I'd be judged by my staff and shouldn't be leaving Khloe and Dan alone. There is no logical reason why I should be feeling that way but that's just how I felt.

Leaving a retail operation and disconnecting kind of feels like dropping off your kid at the babysitters and turning off your cellphone. Regardless of what you're doing, in the back of your mind you know that the store is open and you're never really relaxed. As a parent, you're never really at ease but I needed to learn how to unplug or I was going to lose it.

. . .

The first day on the beach was so weird. I was restless and didn't know what to do with myself. Just lying on the beach felt like a waste of time to me. I wanted my phone and my laptop back but I made a promise to myself to try and centre myself and just work on me.

I grabbed a drink and started looking for a party.

As the days went on, it became easier and easier to unplug. I'd wake up hungover, get food, relax on the beach, and start the process all over again each day. (I really want to give you more details of my entire week but it's a freaking swingers club, man, I just can't.)

By the end of the seven days, I was totally converted. I got the hang of disconnecting and I wanted more of it. I didn't want to come back home or to have my phone and laptop back. I was loving this life too much.

All it took was seven days to convert me.

. . .

When I got back to Montreal from Jamaica, as much as I didn't want to, I had to get right back to work, which I hated so much. I didn't even have time to adjust. My phone was ringing off the hook the second I picked it up from my sister.

Even though I was right back to work, I don't think I ever fully came back from that vacation. My body was in Canada but my mind stayed in Jamaica. I wanted to be back in that free space, that space that had no stresses and no worries. I wanted that escape.

Although I knew that the escape was just a band-aid solution, I still liked it. It was better than the alternative, the stress of the daily entrepreneurial grind.

Since I couldn't go back to Jamaica, I tried to make my own resort life back in Canada. Every weekend, I'd be out at a club partying, drinking and searching for that escape.

In Montreal, I'd usually go out with Tonya but I had a few other women I was dating there as well at the time so I'd just bounce around.

My Toronto lifestyle was a bit different.

My condo in Toronto was smack in the middle of the city, a five-minute walk to the clubs and I think that's what made Toronto a bit different from Montreal where my house was in the suburbs. My lifestyle in Toronto involved less dating and a bit more hooking up which I hated.

During these stressed-out times, I hated being alone with my thoughts. Since I didn't know as many people in Toronto and had no family there, I was out much more than I was in Montreal.

There was no calm for me in Toronto; I had to search for it.

Dating as much as I did wasn't good for my inner self and adding hooking up to it was really fucking draining to my soul.

I hated it, but I didn't stop.

It's like being hungry and craving a steak but the only restaurant around is a McDonald's. (I hate McDonald's btw). I was searching for something, but I couldn't find it.

I wasn't in a good place.

I really thought partying, dating and trying to be overtly wild would help me but they were only fun in the moment. I'd feel so lost in the mornings.

I'm not saying I'd wake up with tears in my eyes or anything like that but I'd wake up feeling emptier. I also felt a bit pathetic, to be honest with you. Here I was this grown-ass man, successful business owner and I couldn't get my shit together. Have you ever felt pathetic about yourself before?

It's an awful feeling; trust me.

Most people are in denial when they are feeling pathetic. Pathetic is a term people use to describe someone else, not themselves, but when you're as low as I was, you can clearly see it and it's not easy to deal with.

I couldn't stay home alone on weekends, and that's pathetic. I had to be out partying and trying to get away from my thoughts all the time. It was either work or party -- there was no middle ground.

I don't know how I ended up here; I wasn't always like this.

When I was modelling or first building Exclucity, I was always alone and I'd be 100% fine with it. I spent almost an entire year in South Africa modelling and I wasn't with one woman out there. I was totally fine alone.

I was living in a model house and there were women all around me, but I was super-focused back then. Nothing could distract me but that wasn't the case now.

Whenever I felt down or lost, I'd call a woman over, we'd have a few drinks and I'd forget about all my worries. It turned into a pattern and what started out as a weekend thing with Tonya soon developed into a nightly routine of drinking, partying and then heading back to my place with a woman.

I couldn't find a balance.

Every day, I'd get up around 7am, go to the gym and then back home to do some work. I'd have a few meetings here and there and then get on my phone to see which woman was free that night. We'd hang out and I'd go to bed around 2-3am and then I'd start the process all over again the next morning.

Some nights, I'd have dinner with one woman and then dessert and drinks with another. There were times that I'd fly back and forth from Montreal and Toronto in a day just to go on multiple dates.

Things got so crazy that I even started edging.

. . .

Even though I was in a bad place, I'm proud that I never let go of my core values. I was always connected to every woman that I was with and we always had a great time together. Most women love laughter, conversation and intelligence. I think having a great conversation with a woman is like foreplay to her and I'm the same way. I'm more like a woman when it comes to picking a partner.

I like flirting over text message during the day, laughing and making jokes, then getting together for dinner and drinks while continuing that banter we started earlier in day. That turns me on.

I love vibing with someone, talking and laughing for hours not even realizing where the time has gone. Both of us are lost in conversation and in each other's space, it's so good.

So, while the actual dating process itself wasn't bad for me, the real problem was that I didn't realize that I was just trying to run away from my depression. I was always searching for something that wasn't there in my personal life and instead of trying to find out what that was, I did the typical thing of burying it and tried to party it away.

I didn't start understanding what was going on until 2018 when I decided to seek therapy, but even then I didn't start really understanding myself until March 16, 2020, when the pandemic hit.

All this time, I thought I was just trying to have fun and figuring myself out. I had no idea that I could have possibly been in and out of manic and hypomanic episodes, and was perhaps suffering from bipolar disorder.

EXCLUCITY 5 | 2017
Tier Zero

2017

Tier Zero

As you may recall, in late 2015, Nike had *Sidelined* Exclucity for the entire year of 2016 so that I could fix my backend, get better operationally, and they also 'suggested" that I step up my store design.

These were all things that I needed to get done one day but I wished it could have been on my own terms and not theirs. But regardless, I got it done.

With all of the above accomplished, *2017* was set up to be Exclucity's comeback year. But before I dive into *2017* and explain to you why things didn't turn out as planned, let me outline a few things first. I need to explain Nike's "suggestions" to you.

One of the first things I did after Nike made a few very expensive "suggestions" to me about my operations team was to hire a headhunter to help me find a controller.

A Controller:

*A **controller** oversees an organization's daily accounting operations, including the accounting, payroll, accounts payable and accounts receivable departments. The **controller** also helps guide a company's strategic financial decisions — and is therefore integral to the financial health of the firm.*

Once I found a controller and that problem was solved, I went out to solve another one of Nike's very expensive "suggestions." I found a designer to create a new store concept for me.

. . .

If I were to blindfold you, walk you into a Starbucks and take it off, you'd know you were inside a Starbucks without seeing the name from the outside. That, my friends, is what we call **Branding**. You know the colours, furniture, look, and feel of the Starbucks stores -- that's what I needed to do with Exclucity.

The Exclucity logo may have been well known, the brand was built but I needed to take that up a notch and brand the actual stores themselves. If Exclucity wanted to expand we needed to be a full brand.

It sounds simple, but all of that cost money, a lot of money.

. . .

I found a small boutique designer in Montreal that specialized in high-end boutique store buildouts and did everything locally and custom-made. They were able to make all the fixtures, benches and furniture to my specifications and with Exclucity's branding, our trademark X, on it. These designers were exactly what I needed. I signed a contract with them and they got to work right away.

Within a few weeks, I flew the entire design team to Toronto to see the stores, their locations and the other retailers in the area. I also took them to every other sneaker boutique in Toronto -- big, small, and everyone in-between. We had meeting after meeting trying to understand Exclucity, the brand, and my concept.

Within a few months, we had a great new concept that I loved and that I felt was ready to be presented to Nike.

The next day I walked into Nike's head office with my new operations team led by my controller, my new action plans, and a 3D walk-through design of the new store ready for presentation.

The Nike leadership team was not only impressed, they were all blown away. It was a great day and just like that I was taken off the bench and allowed to play on the field again.

I was excited but I also had a tremendous amount of anxiety about everything. I had a full expansion plan ready to go but I didn't have a plan on how I was going to pay for it. I just knew that I wanted to make it work and I hoped I'd figure it out along the way.

. . .

No Support

At the end of my presentation, I proposed and asked Nike for approval for my next store to be in Brampton at the Bramalea City Centre, which was approved quickly as Nike loved my new concept, team and direction.

I also asked Nike if I could get more allocations on product, like Retro Jordans and key product drops that sell out quickly, to help offset the added expenses of premium mall rent and a premium store buildout costs.

They told me no.

That has always been my issue with Nike. I think they support their major partners with huge Retro Jordan allocations, but they don't support their regional partners, like Exclucity, the same way. When

Footaction, which is owned by Footlocker, opened their Jumpman door (Jordan store), they opened for 4 days straight, 24 hours per day and allegedly sold $2.5 million worth of Retro Jordan product.

Where the fuck did that Retro Jordan product come from?

It could have only come from one place, Nike Canada -- the same place I get my Jordan product. Where was my increase in Jordan allocation? Where was my support? Do you have any idea how much a fraction of those pairs would have helped me when I was opening my Brampton location?

My biggest issue with Nike's "suggestions" was that Nike wasn't ready to support this action plan with more product allocations. My new stores would now cost me more money to open, but I'd still end up with the same sales totals at the end of the year meaning that I'd have smaller net profit. Nike was allocating me the same amount of product for a 500K store as they would one that was 100k. That made absolutely no sense but I went along with the plan anyways because I knew it was the only way for me to be able to get back in the game.

You can't open a sneaker boutique and not carry Nike. That's like opening a coffee shop and only having orange juice on the menu, it just doesn't make any sense.

Yes, Nike is that dominant in this space!

Regardless of the lack of support from Nike Canada, I pressed on.

. . .

Bad Timing

Within the next few weeks, my design team started production on all of the new furniture and fixtures. I also signed the lease for the Bramalea City Centre and put everything in motion.

It had been exactly a year since I opened any new stores and I was hungry and ready to get back into the game. With my new team in place and approval to open more doors, I started planning out the next phase of my expansion, not realizing I was heading into a disaster.

I planned to open Brampton and then right after that to tear down the first Downtown Toronto location on Queen St. and to redo it with the brand-new store concept. After that, I planned to open one on Yonge St., then in Vancouver, and thereafter the rest of Canada.

I had a full plan in my head but I HAD NO IDEA how the fuck I was going to be able to execute it. Based on the past few years of Exclucity's sales, my expansion plans kind of made sense. But it was extremely risky and required sales to increase for me to be able to pull it all off, which never happened causing a snowball effect that took years to recover from.

In Book 1, I highlighted that 2012 was the biggest year in sneakers and I capitalized off of it. Well, *2017* was the complete fucking opposite and I lost big time.

The Nike and Adidas battle that plateaued in *2017* really hurt Exclucity in a major way, I never saw it coming and it happened at the worst possible time, smack in the middle of my most aggressive and expensive store expansion period.

I should have titled this book, *How Tier Zero Ruined My Life*. Let me explain…

. . .

Tier Zero

This is the part in the book when things start to go bad for me, really bad.

Here we go!

Here's the first verse from "Facts" (Charlie Heat Version) a song off of Kanye West's album "Life Of Pablo."

Yeezy, Yeezy, Yeezy just jumped over Jumpman

Yeezy, Yeezy, Yeezy just jumped over Jumpman

Yeezy, Yeezy, Yeezy, I feel so accomplished

I done talked a lot of shit but I just did the numbers

Herzog and Adidas, man you know they love it

If Nike ain't have Drizzy, man they wouldn't have nothin', woo!

If Nike ain't have Don C, man they wouldn't have nothin', ooh!

But I'm all for the family, tell 'em, "Get your money"

Yeezy, Yeezy, Yeezy, they line up for days

Nike out here bad, they can't give shit away

I stuck to my roots, I'm like Jimmy Fallon

I ain't dropped the album but the shoes went platinum (Woo!)

Every time I talk they say I'm too aggressive

I was out here spazzin', all y'all get the message?

On the field I'm over-reckless, on my Odell Beckham

2020, I'ma run the whole election, yah!

I've been trending years, y'all a couple days

Yeezy in the house and we just got appraised

Nike, Nike treat employees just like slaves
Gave LeBron a billi' not to run away (Yo!)

When Adidas first dropped Yeezys, Ultra Boost and NMDs every single pair was selling out no matter the colour. This was the first time ever that a brand other than Nike was selling out like that. Everyone in the industry was in shock and we were looking to Nike for a response because we knew that they wouldn't just sit back and let this happen. From the day Kanye West left Nike, he had been taking shots at Nike and taking specific aim at Jordan Brand. It was only a matter of time before the upper management would decide to fight back.

A few months after the Adidas onslaught, I finally got the call from Nike that I knew I was going to get at some point. Nike and Jordan Brand were ready to fight back and I was about to find out what the plan was.

Adidas had poked the bear.

My Nike/Jordan sales rep and my new marketplace director called me up and they told me that they wanted to take me out for dinner because Jordan Brand was making some changes and they wanted to fill me in on it.

I was ECSTATIC. I knew something major was going to go down and I knew this dinner was about that. I couldn't wait to find out what it was and how Exclucity would be involved, but when I got to this dinner, I felt like something was a bit off. The guys weren't as fun and relaxed as they usually were with me. I got a funny feeling in my stomach and sensed that they had some bad news for me.

I had no idea I was about to be caught in the crossfire of the Adidas vs Nike battle.

. . .

Since Kanye West and other brands in the industry were leaning more toward high-end fashion, Jordan Brand had decided to add a new layer to their distribution strategy targeted at high-end fashion and called it Tier Zero.

Now, it's important to point out that Tier Zero wasn't a new concept as the Nike footwear division had it for years. It was designated for high-end boutiques and it was built to introduce more trendy designs with high-end materials. It was an elite division within Nike but they never really had any super high-profile releases, one or two a year but that was it.

Jordan Brand was about to take that concept, **blow it the fuck up** and turn the industry upside down on its ass.

Shockingly, my dinner with the Nike/Jordan Canadian leadership team wasn't only to tell me about Jordan Brand's Tier Zero plan to fight back against Kanye and Adidas, it was also to tell me that Exclucity wouldn't be in the distribution plan and wouldn't be receiving any of the Jordan Tier Zero releases.

KNIFE

TO

THE

MIDDLE

OF

MY

FUCKING

HEART!!!!

I couldn't believe what I was hearing. I had just restructured my entire fucking company based on their freaking "suggestions" and this was the result?

I was right in the middle of my very aggressive, expensive, growth plan and two months into it I found out that the biggest brand I carry -- the most profitable brand I sell, the brand I was relying on to turn things around the most so that I could make all my plans work -- is now making major changes to their distribution plan and Exclucity isn't included.

It took every single ounce of my composure that night not to lose my mind in that restaurant and just break all the way down. My entire world, my entire life flashed before my eyes. I swear to you it was like getting hit by a fucking Mack truck. I was frozen for like 30 seconds, my body was numb.

I hate even rethinking about it now while typing this.

. . .

The Nike Canadian leadership said that they tried their best to have me included in the new Tier Zero program but the leadership team back in Beaverton had strict rules. To be part of Jordan Tier Zero, you had to be a high-end boutique carrying certain high-end luxury brands that Exclucity just wasn't carrying.

Exclucity wasn't excluded from Tier Zero because of anything I did wrong. It didn't matter that Exclucity was a great store and that I had been a great partner to Jordan Brand for over 10 years. Exclucity just didn't fit into the "requirement" of the new Tier Zero program and that was it.

We were excluded based on a requirement scale, that's bullshit.

Exclucity had been one of the biggest -- if not the biggest -- regional accounts to sell Jordans in Canada, and Jordan Brand's management just cut me off like I was nothing to them.

I felt betrayed and I felt wronged, but more importantly, I started to panic because I knew this could end Exclucity.

Prior to this new Jordan Brand Tier Zero strategy, any Jordan shoe that got released in Canada came through Exclucity's doors. That's what Exclucity had been known for since the inception of the brand. It's in the name, Exclusive City.

This new Tier Zero offence wasn't only going to cut me out of high-energy product launches, it was also going to hurt the entire regular inline Retro product which was our biggest seller. It's what we depended on to lead our profits and sales. The Nike leadership team didn't realize that in the beginning but I knew that right away. I knew how my clients think and what they want to purchase.

Not having the most sought-after product in the Jordan Brand lineup and having poor Retro Jordan sales are retail suicide for a store like mine. Imagine trying to sleep at night knowing that your brand is drowning and you can't save it.

We were sidelined for an entire year and then moved to creating more expensive stores with the same amount of product allocations. Now, Exclucity was being cut out of top-tier Jordan product.

This pushed me over the edge.

. . .

As much as I tried to hold back most of my emotions in the restaurant, I still voiced my urgent concerns right away. The Canadian leadership team thought I was overreacting and they tried to calm me down by reassuring me that Jordan Tier Zero wasn't going to be that big. They said it wouldn't overshadow the regular Jordan releases that happen most Saturdays. They tried to assure me that it wouldn't affect sales.

But I knew they were wrong. I knew it in my gut.

I got up from the table and called Dan and Khloe. From the second that I told Khloe what was going on, she also started freaking out and said, "We're gonna be fucked." She was shocked and concerned exclaiming, "Jordan and Nike are going to try and fight Adidas and Kanye so hard that all the hot new releases are going to run through Tier Zero and high-end boutiques so that it can be more limited. The kids are gonna go crazy and want those releases more than the regular weekend releases." Those were my sentiments exactly.

I don't know if the Nike Canadian leadership team really thought that Jordan Tier Zero wasn't going to hurt sales of the regular inline Jordan product or if they too were blindsided by Global like I was. But I do know that if I had to do it all over again, I would have trusted my gut and Khloe's intuition and shut down all of our expansion plans that night after the dinner, but I didn't.

I trusted the Canadian Nike team and hoped that Jordan Tier Zero wouldn't affect Exclucity's sales or the overall performance of the Jordan Brand. But that was single-handedly the biggest fucking mistake I ever made in my long entrepreneurial career.

Huge mistake.

Within 6-8 months of this new Jordan Tier Zero strategy, it was clear that the Nike Canadian leadership team was DEAD WRONG. Not following my gut cost me millions of dollars in losses.

I should have listened to my whispers but I couldn't hear them. I kept my expansion plans rolling.

I opened my 7th location at the Bramalea City Centre -- the first store inside a mall -- and from the first month it was not profitable.

Not one month.

Prior to opening that Brampton store, every other Exclucity location had been profitable within the first month and I never lost money. I did not need an investor or a loan and I was able to do it all on my own -- the stores paid for themselves. But all of that was about to change now that I had just experienced my first major loss.

. . .

Nike vs Adidas

The sneaker industry was fucked up.

With Jordan Tier Zero in full swing, Nike and Adidas were going at each other's neck almost every month. Both brands were focused on outdoing each other with special edition, extra limited, and nearly impossible to get releases.

They were both using the same supply and demand strategy that they used prior to this but now it was on steroids. The customers loved it and they went nuts for it.

A client doesn't care where they shop or where they have to go to get their limited releases. They just want their sneakers so they can post it on the gram and then resell it for five times the price on a reselling sneaker app or a consignment store. All this hype was great for the client but bad for retailers and what neither Nike nor Adidas realized at the time was that it was horrible for both of them as well.

I don't think the Global Jordan leadership team realized what they were doing to their own brand. They were actually killing their own inline Retro product because they were so focused on high-end limited Tier Zero releases.

The kids no longer wanted "General Releases," they only wanted limited Tier Zero product. All of a sudden, after 30-plus years of people wearing GRs, they were no longer cool and that killed the sales. We were hurting badly. All of those limited Tier Zero release only benefited one group, the high-end boutiques. Everyone else lost.

Stores like Exclucity lost because we were no longer the cool spots to shop at and both Nike and Adidas did too because they make more money when they can scale a product. Limited is not profitable.

. . .

To end *2017*, Nike put the Adidas attack into overdrive and released the Off-White x Nike "The Ten" Collection, which shocked the entire sneaker world and turned it upside down. It's all anyone spoke about for months. It didn't end the Nike & Adidas battle but it tipped things in Nike & Jordan's favour drastically. For the next two-years, Nike & Jordan kept their foot on the gas and eventually just steam-rolled over Adidas. Nike & Jordan Brand would ultimately be victorious like everyone knew they would.

Now years later, no one cares about Boost, Ultra Boost or NMD. Yeezy is still relevant and there are multiple major drops throughout the year but Boost is dead. And just to be clear, Yeezy never jumped over Jumpman. Yeezy did post up Jumpman, slowed him down, roughed him up in the paint a bit but never jumped over The Jumpman!

. . .

So, what did this mean for Exclucity in **2017**?

Well, not wanting to give up and avoiding the work that I needed to do within myself to make the right decision, I pressed on blindly.

I had invested a lot of money into the new additions that Nike "suggested" and was now having weak Jordan and Nike sales. I was stuck and had no money. I had got myself into a major bind and knew there was no way I was going to be able to make it through the entire year.

Prior to all of this, I had been in business for eleven years, had seven locations and zero debt. The banks used to call me up trying to lend me money and I'd turn them down because I didn't need it but times were changing. I was forced to do something that I had been trying to avoid doing for years.

I was forced to go to the bank and get a loan.

Fuck, I wish I didn't take out those loans. It hurts right now just thinking about it. Loans aren't bad, there is good debt and there is bad debt. But the multi-million-dollar loans that I took out were to cover bad debt and that was a huge fucking mistake.

2017 was the first year, after being in business for more than eleven years, in which I made zero money the entire year and I just broke even.

. . .

I put the bad time of 2017 behind me, took the money for my new loans and put in motion my plans to open a new store at Yonge-Dundas Square in February 2018.

I also signed a lease to open a beautiful store in Vancouver, British Columbia, on Granville St. one of Vancouver's biggest retail hubs, which I scheduled to open for back-to-school in September 2018.

. . .

I thought the past few years were hard on me, but it wasn't until 2018 when I lost $2.23 million, that I fully went over the edge and totally lost myself.

It was like living in a 24/7 nightmare that I couldn't wake up from.

TRENT 6 | 2018
Bipolar

2018

Bipolar

In Book 1, I spoke about my issues with my father in my early teenage years and how our toxic relationship led me to tie one end of my karate belt around my neck and the other to my bedroom door handle before leaning forward.

I was trying to get away.

As a result, I had to start seeing a social worker at my high school on a regular basis and I had to do therapy outside of school. I guess you could say that I've been dealing with mental health almost all my life.

Therapy can help you process things that aren't making sense in your head but it can be a strenuous process if you're not ready to receive it.

Therapy is the clearest mirror you'll ever look into and sometimes you don't want to see everything that clearly because it can be overwhelming.

. . .

2015 to 2018 was really strenuous on me. I had some wins but I had more losses and I was struggling to find myself. My personal life was a complete mess and I just came off an unprofitable business year. I wasn't in a great space mentally.

I had three Exclucity locations in Montreal that weren't profitable, one new location in Brampton that had failed from day one, and a new store on Yonge St. -- with astronomical rent -- that was showing no signs of profitability.

I hired consultants to try and help with the business but they told me that if I continued on this path I wouldn't make it to 2019.

I had daily meetings with Khloe to go over ways we could try and turn things around at the stores but it was really out of our hands. The Nike vs. Adidas battle was having a major effect on the sneaker industry and our sales were down.

The morale of the staff was low, they were unmotivated and Khloe was dropping hints about quitting.

I was in such a dark place. It felt like the walls were closing in on me.

. . .

From the outside looking in, everything was great. I had just bought a huge house in Montreal, my condo in Downtown Toronto was on the top floor with an amazing view of the city and I was always out partying and dating.

I may have been fooling everyone that was watching me but certainly not myself. I knew something was off and although I didn't know what it was exactly, it just didn't feel right. I wanted to talk to someone about it.

I proudly go to a health care clinic that specializes in health promotion, not just health care. They teach you best practices about how **not** to get sick as opposed to regular clinics that only treat you when you're already sick. The clinic also pays very close attention to mental health and it was during my annual check-up that my doctor spotted a red flag.

It started off with questions regarding whether I was getting enough sleep, then others about stress levels, physical activities, time off, time with friends and family, and what kind of social life I had and so on.

After I answered, my doctor was concerned about the dating and drinking of my social life and, of course, my stressful work life.

We decided to have a few weekly sessions to determine if I needed to go see a psychologist or if these issues could be dealt with by us.

I started meetings with my doctor every Wednesday afternoon, but I stopped my sessions after six weeks because work was pulling me away or at least that's the reason I told myself.

. . .

The Breakdown

I was in Paris for a few days for Men's Fashion Week and landed back in Montreal on June 23, *2018.* While I was in my Uber leaving the airport, I opened Instagram on my phone, turned on the camera and said, "I know my life seems exciting. You just saw me partying and living the life in Paris for the past few days, but trust me life is not always as it seems on social media. I'm in a dark place and I'm getting off Instagram for a few months. Bye, I'm out."

After I did that, I changed my Uber destination from my house to the liquor store and then went to Tonya's house because I didn't want to be alone.

When I got to Tonya's house, I didn't want to do anything. I didn't want to talk, I just wanted to drink my rum and lie in bed forever.

I stayed at Tonya's house in her bed for the next five days straight and even though I was in bed for that time, I hardly slept. All I could think about were the stores, my business sinking, and I felt like the world was caving-in on me.

Over the past two years, I knew in my gut that things were bad but I decided to keep pressing on, thinking that if I kept going things would somehow get better.

I had only continued opening more stores because it was the plan and I knew people were watching. I didn't want to look like a failure. When anyone on my team would ask me how I was going to pull off our growth plans even though our sales were bad, I replied, "I'll figure it out like I always do." And I've said that so many times before and pulled things off, but this time things felt different.

I wasn't sure if I could but I never told anyone.

Afraid to face my fears, I ran in the complete opposite direction. I ran to alcohol, to dating, to any place that would take my mind off things, but trying to run away from your stress is like attempting to run away from your own shadow. It's impossible.

. . .

For the next few weeks, I stayed in Montreal to figure out what the fuck I was going to do and how the heck I was going to save my company and not lose everything that I owned. But then things got even worse.

Khloe called and said she needed to talk to me.

We met up the next day and Khloe told me that after careful consideration she was leaving Exclucity to start her own company. It wasn't totally out of the blue, she had been hinting it for months but it was the last thing that I needed to hear at the time. There was no beef or anything like that, she actually wanted me to invest and partner up with her in her new business. But how the fuck could I do that when my own company was literally falling apart around me?

To add more fuel to the fire, a few days after Khloe told me she was quitting, Dan called to tell me that since Khloe was leaving he was thinking of doing the same.

I couldn't believe what I was hearing; I was in shock. I knew that Dan was unmotivated but I really thought he was going to stay and tough it out with me.

Khloe and Dan were vital to Exclucity. Their combined strengths and talents were the sole reason that I was able to step away from my day-to-day tasks and concentrate on our growth plans. With both gone simultaneously, the foundation of Exclucity would be left standing on one leg -- my leg -- and I had enough to hold up on my own. I didn't need any added weight.

. . .

Pressing on

With no money in the bank to run the company properly, sales at the stores at an all-time low, Khloe and Dan leaving, invoices piling up and landlords calling for rent, what did I do?

I did what I always do. I kept pressing on....

Below is my Instagram post from July 19, **2018**, (just 26 days after my post on June 23 saying that I'm off Instagram for a few months).

I'M BACK!!!!

Over the past month, I've stayed away from posting on social media 'cuz I've been trying to work thru some things. I had a huge wake-up call. And what I know for sure is that...I refuse to lose...I refuse to be beaten...I refuse to fold. It's not in my blood or my character to pack up and quit.

Being as open as I can be, I've mentioned that I've been going thru hard times to show you that success doesn't come easy. It's not all fun. It's working 16-hour days. It's hard work. It's being challenged in ways I didn't expect. Success means making the ultimate sacrifice.

Be careful when you pray for success, cause you just might get it.

Yesterday was my birthday and I'm using it to challenge myself, and I'm going to make drastic changes, personally and in business.

I'm giving myself one year to make this happen.

For those of you who have followed and supported EXCLUCITY for the past 11 years...you deserve better and I'm going to make sure that happens. Some major changes are on the way. It might not be perfect from the start, but with my leadership and the amazing staff at Exclucity, we will make the necessary changes that are needed.

Success means making sacrifices. It sometimes comes with a price, but I know for a fact I am willing to pay that price.

Stay tuned for more details!

Thanks for all the well wishes and keeping me positive through my tough times. All your DM's meant a lot.

Love y'all!!

#imback #hardtimes #stress #depressed #gottogetup #fightback #illneverstop #keeppushing #exclucity #xclu

. . .

That post was really NOT healthy!!!

Don't get me wrong. I'm not saying I should have given up. I love that I'm a fighter and that I'm resilient but you can't go through life managing major life issues with resilience alone.

If you read Book 1, you'll know that I had filed for personal bankruptcy years before I started Exclucity. I've been on welfare not once but two times in my life and I was close to being homeless, having to live in an attic and to shower at the YMCA.

Throughout my entire life, I've been fighting back with resilience but never looked within myself to try and understand why I was always in these situations. Why did I always end up in these highly stressful and life-altering situations that had glaring ups and downs? My journey includes living in the craziest of places, basements, rat-infected attics and always jumping from idea to idea. When they fail, its ok, boom, I have another idea.

I had had enough. I couldn't sleep, rest or think straight and there was no peace in my life. I was getting drunk every night and that wasn't even enough anymore. It felt like I was living in a straitjacket and I couldn't move. My business was collapsing around me and it was suffocating me. It was cutting off my circulation and I couldn't feel my limbs; I was numb. My business was no longer giving me the freedom that it once did; it was crippling me. *Sneakers* may have *Saved My Life* years ago but that was a distant memory now, far in my rear-view mirror.

A few short years after reaching the pinnacle of success, sneakers were no longer my saviour. *Sneakers* had now *Ruined My Life.*

I needed help.

. . .

On August 21, *2018*, I started seeing one of Montreal's leading psychologists and after a few months of weekly sessions it was suggested that **I may be** experiencing hypomanic episodes, while having past (and more severe) manic episodes, and both are often linked to bipolar disorder.

Bipolar:

Bipolar disorder, previously known as manic depression, is a mental disorder characterized by periods of depression and periods of abnormally elevated mood that last from days to weeks each. If the elevated mood is severe or associated with psychosis, it is called mania; if it is less severe, it is called hypomania. During mania, an individual behaves or feels abnormally energetic, happy, or irritable, and they often make impulsive decisions with little regard for the consequences. There is usually also a reduced need for sleep during manic phases.

During periods of depression, the individual may experience crying and have a negative outlook on life and poor eye contact with others.

Hypomania:

Hypomania (literally "under mania" or "less than mania") is a mood state characterized by persistent disinhibition and mood elevation (euphoria), with behaviour that is noticeably different from the person's typical behaviour when in a non-depressed state.

According to DSM-5 criteria, hypomania is distinct from mania in that there is no significant functional impairment; mania, by DSM-5 definition, does include significant functional impairment.

While hypomanic behaviour often generates productivity and excitement, it can become troublesome if the subject engages in risky or otherwise inadvisable behaviours, and/or the symptoms manifest themselves in trouble with everyday life events.

Hypomania may be diagnosed if:

- *A distinct period of elevated or irritable mood occurs in which the mood is clearly different from a regular nondepressed mood.*
- *Three or more of the following symptoms last for a significant period of time:*
- *Inflated self-esteem or unrealistic feelings of importance*
- *Decreased need for sleep (feels rested after only a few hours of sleep)*
- *Talkativeness*
- *Racing thoughts or flight of ideas*
- *Being easily distracted*
- *An increase in goal-directed activity (work or personal)*
- *Irresponsible behaviours that may have serious consequences, such as going on shopping sprees, engaging in increased sexual activity, or making foolish business investments*

- *The mood or behaviour change is noticeable to others.*
- *The episode is not severe enough to cause impairment in social or job functioning and does not require hospitalization.*
- *The symptoms are not caused by substance use.*
  *Michigan Medicine: University Of Michigan

. . .

While no one can ever know for sure, my psychologist thinks that I could have been suffering from bipolar disorder since I was a young teen and it went undetected until now. This meant that when I tied the karate belt around my neck, I could have been experiencing one of my first manic episodes but we'll never know.

A bipolar diagnosis isn't like testing for cancer. You can't just run a few tests and get a positive or negative result the next day. Mental health diagnosis can be very complicated and it's often subjective.

Whether or not the diagnosis was suggestive, I couldn't help but think that maybe my life could have been different.

Perhaps if I had stayed in therapy as a young teen, my life would not have been so challenging. Maybe I would have avoided all this pain, avoided all the horrible shit that happened in my life.

Maybe my entire life would have been different.

Maybe.

EXCLUCITY 6 | 2018
Losing $2.23 Million

2018

Losing $2.23 Million

2018 was going to be my most challenging year in business to date. My sales were on a steady decline and everyone on my upper management team was unmotivated and kind of lost. We were all in limbo and needed inspiration.

I thought of bringing in a consultant or someone from the outside to help lift everyone's spirit and provide us with some fresh ideas, but that's easier said than done when you're running a sneaker boutique.

Running a sneaker company is very different from operating a typical business because it is a unique and niche sector that most entrepreneurs will never understand.

Try telling a regular businessperson that your best-selling products are limited and there is nothing you can do to get any more of it, NOTHING! And not only is the amount you can order limited but it's allocated to you, meaning you have zero say in the process. You get what you get and that's it.

Nothing that I just said above makes any sense but this is the nature of the sneaker business.

Nike and Adidas's supply and demand strategy (in the fashion arm of their business) was very different from, for example, Apple.

Apple makes an iPhone, then promotes and sells as many units as it possibly can until the phone stops selling. The following year the company adds another camera, makes the phone two millimetres larger and sell it to us as a brand-new phone that's bigger and better than every other iPhone before it, and then Apple starts the process all over again.

The same formula is repeated every year.

Most business people only understand the Apple model and rightly so, it's the more lucrative of the two models. But this is why it was so hard for me to find outside help when my business was taking a downturn and my sales were down.

I had always been very reluctant to use consultants because most of them look at things from a high level focusing on fundamental business practices. Since I could foresee that I was about to have financial losses in 2018, I thought it was best to have someone help me manage through it. I knew that a regular consultant couldn't really help me with all aspects of my business but they could with money management and operational practices.

. . .

We started consulting at the end of March **2018** and had two sessions over the next two months. People on my management team were getting things off of their chest, being very open and it helped a lot with the morale. Things were working out very well, just as I had hoped.

These sessions also started to reveal something that I didn't want to face. I know the company was in bad shape but it was in far worse shape than I wanted to admit to myself. Things started to become more and more shocking as we went on.

One of the first things the consultants said was that I should rethink my plans of opening a store in Vancouver in August. They thought it could be detrimental to the business and may bankrupt us. The sales just weren't there.

When the consultants said that to me a few people from my staff turned and looked at me with that "I told you so" face.

I looked right back at them and said, "Oh, hell no, that isn't an option." I've been busting my ass for the past three years to have Nike approve my west coast expansion plans. There was no way that I was going back to them now to say, "Sorry, I'm not opening in Vancouver anymore." That's not going to happen.

The consultants understood and they continued working. After the session, no one said anything about Vancouver again because they knew that it was off the table.

. . .

On **May 4, 2018,** I got a text from James Patterson, an old business associate in Philadelphia. He was the CEO of a major sneaker store in the US that his parents founded and opened more than 30 years ago, they had over 130 locations with sales of $250 million.

James wasn't texting me about business but wanted a list of hotspots for parties in Montreal his teenage son could check out on a visit that weekend. When I sent it, he replied, "Thanks a lot Trent, btw how's business?"

"HORRIBLE," I answered.

James knew first-hand what I was going through as he, like many owners of sneaker stores that weren't high-end, was going through the same thing. The sneaker business was bad all over.

For James and his family, things were worse because they had investors that had a controlling majority in the company. The investors wanted out of the sneaker business and sold the entire company in a merger to another competing sneaker store. Unfortunately, the new sneaker company didn't keep James on as CEO and he was now out of work.

Knowing that James wasn't working at the time he was texting me, I asked him how he was coping with no longer being in the sneaker business after basically growing up in it since he was a teenager. It's all he'd ever known.

His reply was exactly what I thought it would be. He was missing it and we both immediately started thinking along the same lines. We continued texting, then jumped on a call, and James booked a flight to come to Montreal and Toronto to see if he could help me turn things around at Exclucity.

. . .

In 2014, Jim Woods (senior director at Nike, read Book 1 for more details on him) connected James and I together because James and his investors were looking to expand into Canada. Jim had suggested that they should buy Exclucity given the great footprint that we already had in Canada.

The deal never worked out but James and I had always stayed in contact and developed a great relationship.

Seeing that James almost bought Exclucity, he was familiar with the brand already making it easy for us to work together. It was a natural choice.

James came on board as a consultant but because of our relationship we both knew he would be more hands-on than just consulting. He was determined to help me navigate this crucial time as he and his family had a similar experience when they owned ten stores and ultimately had to give up controlling interest to investors just to keep the doors open. If anyone knew how I was feeling during this time and the position that I was in, it was James, not to mention his extensive knowledge and background in the sneaker business.

He was the perfect person for the job.

. . .

June 16, 2018 -- James officially joined the Exclucity team and we hit the ground running. Over the first few days, things were running smoothly. We went over reports, operations, budgets, plans, etc., but after a while James called me to say that he was booking a flight to come back to Montreal to talk to me.

We were scheduled to have our third meeting with the first consultants in a few days so I suggested that James come down the same day so that we could all talk together.

He agreed.

June 28, 2018 -- Just 12 days after joining the team, James literally saved me from making the biggest mistake in my career and helped me save Exclucity.

Here's how.

. . .

Before inviting James to sit in on our meeting, we had an entire day planned out with the consulting firm. The objective was to go over our five-year plan and then onto what our overall mission and goals were, our growth plans, roll out, etc. It was scheduled to be a packed day.

The consultants started off with a nice presentation and they attempted to paint a rosy picture of the next five years. But within the first hour, you could see that they were struggling and that there were holes in the plan; the numbers weren't adding up because we were trending down, **not up**.

At the time, I had agreed to overlook this downtrend assuming that opening up in Vancouver would bring us new business, increase our sales, and would in turn trend our numbers back up.

That was my plan.

I was the only one in the room that was thinking that way but no one said anything at the time because they knew I'd shut it down. This wasn't the first time we had this discussion.

We all sat through the presentation and then broke for lunch.

During that time, some went outside for some fresh air and others chose to eat in other rooms. But then I saw a group of people whispering outside the conference room. It looked like they were having their own little side meeting. I thought it was a bit weird but I didn't think much of it and kept on eating my sushi.

As soon as lunch was over and we were about to start the second half of our day, that's when I found out the purpose of the meeting outside the room. They weren't discussing how great the sushi was but instead planned an intervention.

. . .

James got up and said, "Trent, do you mind if I pause what we are doing so I can show you a few things?" I replied, "Yeah, sure James, go ahead" because in the back in my mind I knew exactly what he was going to say. I was sure that he was going to say something about my expansion plans or say something about Vancouver and I had heard it all a million times before and had all my rebuttals ready. But I was wrong, that's not what happened at all.

This is the moment that Oprah was talking about.

This is when the entire brick wall was about to come crashing down on me. This was my worst nightmare coming true. This is the moment that I had been trying to fight since Nike told me Jordan Brand was changing their distribution strategy with Tier Zero. I knew this could have happened but I was just trying to avoid it.

James very bluntly said, "Trent, if you keep going down this path, you're going to have to file for bankruptcy before the end of the year. I can guarantee you that with the utmost, unequivocal competency."

His voice got deeper and stern. Then he said, "**We need to stop talking about your 5-year plan RIGHT NOW** and start talking about **your 6-month plan** if you want a chance in hell at saving your business. If you don't, you'll be done before Christmas 2018. I can promise you that."

I was stunned and frozen like a deer caught in the headlights.

James continued without me getting a word in, "You need to close down some of your stores **immediately**, with no hesitation. You need to make some very drastic changes right now, today. Not next week or next month, but right now if you want to have even a slim chance, and very slim chance, at surviving all of this."

. . .

Everyone in the room, including the other consultants, had suggested this to me before, but not with this much certainty. I don't know if it was because of James's 25 years of experience in the sneaker business or the fact that everyone in the room was collectively staging this intervention, but I knew it was time to start listening to them.

I knew it was time to put aside my "I can hustle my way through anything, I'm resilient." attitude and start the actual repair process that day. It wasn't easy to do it but I did it right then and there because I knew it was the right thing to do. I grasped very quickly that time was of the essence; there was no time to deliberate.

We scrapped the rest of the afternoon's presentation and started brainstorming and making a plan to fix the Exclucity brand.

It was time to start closing some stores.

. . .

Our first order of business was to stop the bleeding.

Within a few hours, we easily identified three Exclucity locations that were not profitable. I immediately emailed my lawyers and asked them to help me get out of my leases.

Next, I had to make a decision about Vancouver.

I refused to let go of my plans to open the Vancouver location, but I agreed to revisit it in a few months after we closed the three stores, hoping that we'd be in a better financial situation then.

The next issue was, what about the other location that we just opened?

My team and I weren't 100% sure what to do with the Yonge St. and Brampton stores which were both new. I had invested close to a million dollars into them and we weren't sure if they had been given a fair shot at being successful. We agreed that it was way too early to know so we decided to put all of our resources behind them to try to turn things around.

. . .

Discounting Inventory

While the team and I were deep diving into and brainstorming our many issues, we also discovered a huge inventory issue with our Nike product that was killing my cash flow.

Typically, a healthy retail store has 50-60% of its inventory in the current season at regular price, 20%-30% from the season that just ended on a slight discount, and 10% should be from two seasons ago or older. That inventory should be on heavy liquidation and out the fucking door.

My Nike inventory was flipped backwards from the standard practice. Seventy per cent of my inventory was from three seasons ago or older, only 20% from last season, and 10% was from the current season.

That's a horrible ratio.

In the sneaker business, hype sells out right away, then the high-energy product moves out over a few days but then regular product just sits there. It's hard to sell regular product even on discount, especially in the present "hype" era.

Whenever I had sales, what inventory do you think was selling out first? It was the newer product, obviously, and guess what happened when I kept having sales over and over again? The new product would sell out but we'd never sell any of the old ones. They just kept piling up and that was killing my cash flow and drowning the company.

Once we identified the inventory problem, we tried running hundreds of different scenarios to fix it but it all came to the same conclusion. Even though I had made the decision to start closing stores, the reports were telling us that I wouldn't have enough cash on hand to make it to the end of 2018.

All of the reports came to the same reality.

With the next few months of low projected sales, lack of money in the bank, past invoices due, rent, salaries, and outstanding loans, I was 60-90 days away from closing down all Exclucity locations permanently and filling for bankruptcy.

There was no option left on the table for me within my immediate circle. I was tapped out, having already maxed out all my loans, line of credit and credit cards. I needed a Hail Mary or outside help if I was going to make it through this situation. There was only one option left on the table for me and that was to call the company that helped build Exclucity.

I called Nike.

. . .

Wednesday, July 25, 2018

The Nike Canada leadership team was well aware of my financial issues in 2017 and early 2018. I had always been very transparent with them and they had helped me prior to this by delaying some invoice due dates, but their patience was running thin. I was nervous about bringing up the possibility of bankruptcy to their attention. But I had no choice and had to make the call.

I called my marketplace director on July 25, *2018,* and told him that I needed to come in for an emergency meeting and that I'd be bringing James with me.

He agreed and we met the next day.

I wish I never made that call.

. . .

That first meeting with the director was amazing because he understood the situation I was in and acted right away. When I told him that I was only 60-90 days away from closing down all of my locations, he stopped the meeting. He asked me to email him all of my Nike inventory along with sell through reports and to summarize the position I was in, detailing the possibility of bankruptcy.

"Trent, you've been a longtime Nike partner and you've always been an ally to the brand," he said. To reassure me, he continued, "I don't want to see Exclucity closedown. I can't make you any promises but we do have levers that we can pull in these kinds of situations. I'll try my best to buy you some more time to hopefully turn things around. I'll have to discuss all of this with the Nike senior management team but I'll get back to you in a few days, either way."

The urgent call to action and no-nonsense tone of the meeting were promising or at least I thought so.

. . .

The next few nights after our meeting I barely slept. I kept checking my email every hour on the hour, then on July 27, *2018*, just two days after our meeting, I received an email with the subject line......... *Financial Restructure Plan, the next steps.*

NIKE

HAD

MY

BACK,

BUT THEN THEY CUT MY KNEES FROM UNDERNEATH ME.

Step 1 of my Nike Financial Restructure Plan was great. It helped a lot BUT there was a part 2 to that email that came a few weeks later and it rocked my world.

Nike had given me room to breathe for a few months, but they also made devastating changes to the terms of my Nike account that would stop the flow of my orders from shipping out. These critical changes to my account would cause Exclucity to miss key Nike and Jordan launch product that is the foundation of our business. They would also cause my inventory levels to be extremely low at all of my locations. In my opinion, it was like Nike was throwing me a life jacket with holes in it.

To me, this is what the conversation sounded like.

Nike: "Hey Trent, here's a life jacket for you but it has some big fucking holes in it. It will definitely just weigh you down as you tread water and try to survive but hey, at least we threw you something. Don't say we didn't help you.

"Good luck out there, we're driving off now."

Trent: "Hey, wait a second!!! Thanks a lot for the life jacket but can I just get in the boat with you since this life jacket is fucked? Wouldn't that make more sense and everything a lot easier?"

Nike: "Ya, no, sorry about that, Trent. We got **all** the major accounts in the boat with us already. We're busy helping them and there just isn't enough room in here for you.

"Sorry buddy, but good luck."

Trent: "But wait…. Remember back in the day when Nike Basketball wasn't really trending in Canada and I helped lay down the foundation in this country so those major accounts that are in the boat with you could open basketball stores in Canada? I helped with that when no one else really wanted to… remember that???

"Oh also, do you remember when sneaker culture was underdeveloped in Canada back in the day and we worked together to help change the narrative and develop the territory? Y'all remember that? Can I just please come onto the boat?"

Nike: "……………."

Trent: "Hello, Nike? Can you guys hear me….Helloooooo…….."

(End of scene…. Nike drives off in the boat with all the major accounts)

. . .

Nike is a fucking powerhouse and could have done so many different things to help Exclucity out if they really wanted to. They could have upped my allocations on key release product to drive sales and that would have been a major help. They could have gotten me on the Tier Zero program, which would have been a game changer right away!

Nike **did** help me out a bit, I want to make that clear BUT they also fucked me at the same time.

With the new terms of my account, I'd have to pay invoices before they were due just to get product released and shipped. I no longer had enough room to operate normally. I could only get a fraction of my orders released, meaning I'd miss out on profit, which is what I needed the most at the time. It was a vicious cycle.

But it gets worse.

On top of the new terms, Nike added another hole in my fucking life jacket. They put me on "Credit Hold" which means that no Nike/Jordan product would ship AT ALL until I emailed and checked in with someone weekly, sometimes, a couple times a week. The person who I had to check in with would make sure that my account was in good standing and ask me which orders I'd like to release. It was only then that my Nike/Jordan orders would be released.

Nike was very much aware that my cash flow and cash on hand were low. They knew the chances of me surviving with these new changes were next to impossible, but that's how they get you to close down your store while they look good in the process.

It wasn't much different from Adidas.

It was as if Adidas was saying, "Let Exclucity die, what do we care," but Nike was saying, "Oh shit, you're in the hospital in intensive care? Sorry to hear that. We're going to come see you and bring you something to ease the pain as you die a slow death."

In my opinion, neither of them really cared, Nike was just slicker about it.

Regardless of everything that was going on with my suppliers, I really tried my best not to let it break me down. I knew what I was up against and I pressed on; I was determined to not let their bigger plan of seeing me closedown become a reality.

It was time for me to fix my brand on my own.

. . .

Restructuring

Here's the part of the book where I show you how I *lost $2.23 million* in one year. But first, let me explain to you how losing money on a financial statement works, in case some of you don't know. Then I'll try to show you how losing money could help in the rebuilding process.

It's called Restructuring.

Let's assume you have a company and your year-end financial date is December 31, 2017. You buy a pair of shoes during the month of November 2017 for $150. As an example, let's just say the shoes do not sell and stay in your inventory past December 31, 2017 (past your year-end). That $150 will show up on your financial statement for 2017 as an asset.

Now staying with that same example but now it's 2018 and that pair is just sitting on the shelf. They are ugly, nobody wants to buy them so you put them on liquidation and you sell them for only $50 (a $100 loss). On your 2018 financial statement, that $50 that you got from the sale goes towards your sales (cash flow), but you lost $100 so now that $100 loss moves out of the asset column and will now show up as a loss on your 2018 financial statement.

Inventory losses only show up on your financial statement **after** the sale is completed. If you keep the shoes that you bought in 2017 in your inventory for the entire year of 2018 they will stay in your asset column.

Now, take that simple example above of the pair of shoes and multiply them by a shitload more and that's how I lost $2.23 million in one year. Let's just say that I had **a lot** of shoes in inventory that were just sitting on my shelf and in my asset column in 2017 that I liquidated in 2018. They were now showing up as a loss on my 2018 year-end financial statement.

. . .

Here's how I liquidated all those shoes.

In mid-August **2018**, a few weeks after the intervention, we closed down two Exclucity locations and turned one location into a liquidation centre for a month before closing it permanently. We moved the inventory from those two stores to the liquidation store and also brought **all** the old/dated inventory from the remaining stores as well.

It was pandemonium.

I rented 26 ft trucks and made trips from Montreal to Toronto dropping off thousands of pairs of shoes at the liquidation store. I'd drop off trucks full of shoes to the staff that would unload them and then I would pick up more in Montreal and repeat the process. It was pure madness.

We had well over 20,000 pairs of shoes and I marked them all down below cost to move them out quickly. It was mass hysteria at that liquidation store.

We had line-ups daily for almost the entire month that the liquidation store was open. Shoes that were regularly $150 to $250 were now marked down to $30-$60. Members of staff were buying multiple pairs of shoes at a time and they were calling their families and friends to come and shop, it was seriously crazy.

Everyone loved it, everyone except me, of course. I don't think anyone stopped to think what was really going on.

The staff just saw the daily sales totals and assumed that because the dollar amounts were high we were making tonnes of money. They did not realize that with every item that was being sold I was losing a lot of money. With every sale, I was losing $50-$150 per pair of shoes and $20-$60 on clothing.

I was losing tens of thousands of dollars per day. It was like turning on a faucet and watching my money just go down the fucking drain.

I'd go into the store daily to check on things and I'd have to keep a positive attitude trying to keep the staff motivated. But as soon as I'd get back into my car and I was alone, I'd have a breakdown.

I knew that I had a plan, I was restructuring and trying to save the company but I was still so scared that it might not work and that I could lose everything. I knew it would take a few years to fix everything if I were to make it out of this, but I didn't know if I was going to make it. It was really a dark time for me.

I can now assume that perhaps these moments were all triggering moments for me, but at the time I had no idea about bipolar or manic episodes. I didn't know what to do with my emotions. I just felt raw and numb. Alcohol was the only thing that made me feel normal and centred.

. . .

It was a horrible time. I wasn't just losing money but also the two people that helped me make Exclucity what it is today.

Khloe's last day was August 19, *2018*, and Dan's was on August 30, *2018*. Within weeks of closing three Exclucity locations and in the middle of losing tens of thousands of dollars per day, my closest team members were leaving.

I think losing them put me in a depression or a deeper manic state. Yes, I had opened Exclucity five years before hiring them but they both were such a major part of the brand. I wasn't sure how I was going to manage without them.

August 21, **2018** -- Just two days after Khloe quit, I started going to therapy. (I mentioned this date in the previous section)

The therapy sessions were weekly and while I was really trying my hardest to work on myself, I also had a company that needed rescuing. It was hard to prioritize both but like always, I put myself aside and focused on the store, regardless of my diagnosis of possibly being bipolar.

I had four more months to finish out **2018** and now adding to the stress of *losing $2.23 million* and Khloe and Dan, I had to resume running the day-to-day operations at the stores because there was no one left that had that experience.

Coming back to run operations was a nightmare for me because I was unplugged from that part of the business for a few years now. I was lost and it added to my stress but there was one person, who saved my ass.

Enter Keisha!

. . .

Keisha

Keisha was Khloe's assistant and had been working for Exclucity for close to four years. She knew the ins and outs of our entire operation, having started out on the floor as a sales associate and worked her way up in the company. Keisha was smart, capable and eager. While she was really sad to see her mentor, Khloe, leave, she also knew that she had a great opportunity in front of her.

Khloe's position was now open.

Had it not been for Keisha's willingness to step up and learn and help me run Exclucity's day-to- day operations, I really don't know what I would have done. I'm not sure if I would have made it through the year. There were things that Khloe did that I had no idea how to do. She had been running operations for almost three years but Keisha knew most of it and it saved my life.

I promoted Keisha a few days after Khloe left and gave her a raise. We both planned a new strategy to rescue Exclucity and we set out to accomplish it.

I had to put myself and my mental state aside, I felt like I had no choice. It was either work on me or work on saving Exclucity. The answer was always the same.

Save Exclucity and worry about me later.

. . .

In her new management position, Keisha would now be able to implement ideas that she couldn't while an assistant to Khloe. She had been working on the floor directly with the customers and knew them well. She also had brilliant ideas on what to do with the staff, like changing outdated employee policies, etc. Keisha was the breath of fresh air that I needed.

She had no idea at the time but she was carrying Exclucity on her back during a time that I couldn't hold up that much weight.

I was just a few weeks into therapy and trying to figure things out. I was still running to a different woman's house each night because I couldn't be alone, was afraid to face my demons and continued to drown my pain and stress away in bottles of alcohol.

If Keisha didn't step up the way she did, I don't know where I'd be today.

. . .

Keisha and I worked really hard for a few weeks on a strategic plan to make drastic changes to try and help save Exclucity.

We spent a full week visiting all of the remaining Exclucity locations in Montreal and Toronto. We had meetings with all the store managers and told them that there would be some major changes coming down the pipeline. We advised them to sit tight because things were about to change for the better.

After I worked with Keisha for a few weeks, I left her to be on her own and switched my attention to other parts of my upper management team.

I initially hired a buyer and an assistant buyer, and a few months later an E-commerce manager and a social media manager.

A few weeks after all those hires, Keisha and I rented a big conference space in Toronto for a meeting with all the Toronto staff. We brought everyone together, the upper management and staff from all the stores, even the stock boys. Soon after, I did the same with the Montreal staff.

At both of these conferences Keisha and I detailed our new plans, polices and overall new direction for the company. I also filled everyone in on my new long-term plans of not opening anymore brick-and-mortar stores and dedicating more resources to online.

I was running our offence through a new and improved lens and I wanted to share it with them.

. . .

After months of meetings, strategizing and planning, it was now time to implement all these new ideas and strategies. I gave Keisha a target that she had to hit for us to have a fighting chance and for us to make it in 2019. I told her that we didn't just need to hit these sales numbers, but it was a **must** that we hit them or else we'd have to close.

Keisha immediately got to work, rallied her team and they not only hit their targets but they beat them. I knew Keisha was a superstar but I was blown away by her work ethic, grit and passion for success.

She really stepped up in a major way.

. . .

Being in therapy weekly during the last half of *2018* was revealing, terrifying and also very confusing. Having a liquidation sale that moved millions of dollars from my asset column into my net loss column felt like losing a kidney and losing Khloe and Dan felt like surgically removing one of my lungs.

2018 had been one of the most horrible years in my life. I had critical losses and was on life support but I learned more about business, the people around me, and myself than I did in any other year.

I survived 2018.

TRENT 7 | 2019
Spiraling Out of Control

2019

Spiraling Out of Control

They say when you survive a near-death experience you automatically start looking at life differently. Exclucity wasn't supposed to make it to *2019*, but through the grace of God, an amazing staff and some really hard work we made it. Barely, but we made it.

Regardless of the company's survival, I knew I was in for a hell of a year. *2019* wasn't going to be much different from the previous year. Exclucity was basically in a hold position -- hold on to see what the fuck was going to happen.

The team and I had stopped the bleeding and now it was time for us to tread water and just try to stay afloat as long as possible without drowning. James had given Exclucity a 5-10% chance at survival, which was so hard to wake up and fight for each day.

I could not put into words how that felt and I didn't know how to deal with it.

The stress of staying still and slowly watch my company potentially die was too much for me. It's like watching someone battle a life-threatening disease and you don't know if they will live or die.

How did I manage through it?

I just pretended like nothing was happening and kept marching on.

I didn't want to sit by Exclucity's bedside and watch it die a slow death. I wanted to check in and visit once in a while, do what I could do and keep it moving.

If there were a 50-50 chance at survival, then yes, I'd be more invested, even a 20-30%, but a 5-10% chance was too much to bear at the time.

I was too weak.

I remember thinking, "Maybe this is what a manic episode is, not caring or being detached and not caring about the outcome." I had no idea and I didn't care. I didn't want to know. I didn't even want to talk about it at therapy. One day my therapist brought up hypomania and I said, "Let's not go there and lets not talk about the store either. I don't want to talk about it."

Afraid to face my fears and not being able to stop myself from thinking nightly about potentially losing everything that I owned, I turned to the things that made me feel good and gave me comfort: partying, alcohol and dating.

That's how I dealt with my stress. At the time I didn't want to deal with it any other way.

•**February 4, 2019** -- I went to Las Vegas for a retailer trade show but I didn't go with James, the Exclucity buyers or anyone from my team, I brought a woman from Toronto that I had been dating for a few months.

We landed in Vegas at 10pm and we didn't leave the hotel room for the first 24 hours. We spent the next three days in Vegas but attended the trade show for only a few hours. Most of our time was spent at parties, restaurants and strip clubs, then right back to the hotel room.

•**February 24, 2019** -- I went to Barbados with two of my boys. We rented out a 4-bedroom penthouse with two balconies, a hot tub and a killer view. The property was on the famous Barbados strip.

The first night we went out I met a beautiful Bajan woman and I was drunk every night.

•**March 13, 2019** -- I went to an all-inclusive resort in Jamaica with Tonya.

. . .

I had no idea what was going to happen with Exclucity and did not have a solid plan on how to save it. I was just off doing my thing trying to manage through it.

In my head I knew that I had tried everything possible over the past few years so it was time to just deal with whatever the outcome could be.

The sale numbers were still very low at each location and I had no money in the bank. We were just barely scraping by but I did whatever I could do to not focus on that.

I started coming up with some outside the box ideas.

•**May 2, 2019** -- I posted this on my Instagram:

NEW SHOW ALERT: I'm finally back in front of the camera where I belong. I'm stepping out from behind the desk, getting out of the store and I'm hitting the road with a brand-new show on IGTV and YouTube titled: Trent Out Loud

I'll be hitting up fashions shows, concerts, restaurants, festivals, etc. Anything that has to do with our culture, I'll be there covering it. I'll also be doing 1-on-1 interviews with fashion designers, rappers/singers and bringing you behind the scenes of streetwear brands. We're going around the world, NYC, LA, TOKYO, PARIS, etc. It's gonna be a crazy ride, TRUST ME!!! Stay tuned, keep it locked, this is just the beginning.

Anddddd thank you for all the love and support, I appreciate it so much!

I know this might sound shocking to you but my Trent Out Loud idea was my brilliant plan on how to make money if I had to close down Exclucity and file for bankruptcy.

I honestly have no idea what I was thinking at the time.

Was this hypomania? Was it mania?

Mania brings on intense energy, racing thoughts and creative ideas mixed with extreme and exaggerated behaviours while having no fear of the consequences of such behaviours.

Hypomania is being in a state of mind when you're feeling super creative, positive, uplifted and feeling like you can do anything but you can see the consequences of your actions and as a result you don't take major risks.

Some days, I'd be focused on trying to save Exclucity, but most days it took a backseat to Trent Out Loud. What the hell did that mean?

Was I bipolar or was I just fed up of beating my head against the same wall and expecting a different result?

I had no idea because I quit therapy.

. . .

Quitting Therapy

I cancelled my May 3, *2019,* therapy session and never went back. I was simply focused on having fun, vacationing, drinking and partying. I started smoking weed and was not sleeping much. All I wanted to do was work on Trent Out Loud, the show was my main focus.

In one of my last therapy sessions before I quit, I said to my psychologist, "Although I was very happy that I still had my company, I really didn't care if Exclucity didn't make it through 2019. I was so fed up of the ups and downs of the past few years and thought Trent Out Loud would make me way more money in the long run."

I told him that I didn't need Exclucity as long as I had my Trent Out Loud platform.

Comments like those were red flags to my psychologist. I remember him asking me, "Are you currently making any money off of your Trent Out Loud platform? And if you're not, what will you do for money? How will you pay for your house?"

"That's actually what's driving me, it pumps me up. Maybe this is the push that I need to make Trent Out Loud really work. Who cares if I'm not making money off the platform right now? I'm not scared to lose my house. If I need money, I'll go out and be a janitor on the night shift, I don't care. I've been a janitor before, I'll do it again if I have to," I replied.

It was comments like these that made my therapist think that perhaps I was manic.

Before I quit therapy, my psychologist and I discussed hypomania a few more times. While he didn't think I needed to take medication, he suggested that I tell someone in my family or a friend so that I would have support.

He thought by telling me about the possibility of hypomania and mania that I'd be more aware and use my support system around me.

Here's where that plan fucked up.

Since I didn't take the recommendation regarding hypomania that seriously at first, I diverted from the plan and didn't tell a single person in my family or any of my close friends. The only person that I told was Tonya so that there was at least one person in this world that knew about it, in case anything happened to me.

I was reluctant to tell my family because they are old school Jamaicans who don't fully understand mental health and therapy. I kind of told my sister about it but she just brushed it off and said, "Ya, I can see how you could be hypomanic but I don't think you are."

I didn't even consider telling my dad about it. I knew for sure he'd do the same as my sister.

My mom was the only person that I really wanted to tell but I was worried that she'd be stressed out as usual. She's way too old school to want to deal with mental health and would have probably said, "Your doctor is wrong, Trent. You look fine. I really don't think there is anything wrong with you."

As if you can see mental health on someone's face like how you can tell if someone has a fever or the flu.

. . .

Fresh off quitting therapy and feeling like I was on top of the world, I dropped my first episode of Trent Out Loud. Every other week, I dropped a new episode. Over the next six months, I put all my efforts into that show.

- I dropped my first episode of Trent Out Loud on IGTV filmed outside my Yonge St. store. I asked people that were walking by trivia questions about the upcoming Jordan 4 Retro "Bred" release. The first one that got all 5 questions right won a free pair of Jordan 4 "Breds."

- I got tickets for all three home games to the Toronto Raptors Eastern Conference Finals and did an episode where I asked fans trivia questions about the team outside of the ACC.
- I did an episode with the Centre for Addiction and Mental Health (CAMH).
- I did an episode at a Sneaker Convention.
- I covered the 2019 Raptors Finals win over the Golden State Warriors. The show starts off with me on top of a bus in the middle of Yonge St. with about 200 people alongside me and thousands on the street.
- I did a show with Complex and Lotto Max.
- I interviewed Jeff Staple.
- I interviewed Conceited from MTV's "Wild 'n Out."
- I covered Montreal's Grand Prix weekend.
  And lastly,
- I covered Toronto's Caribana Parade.

Along with all these episodes, I also did podcasts, events, speaking engagements, interviews and whatever else I could find that would elevate my new Trent Out Loud platform.

Trent Out Loud was my new major focus in life. I really thought it would become huge one day.

I hired a camera guy to follow me around almost daily. There was a photographer on call for events and speaking engagements and I also had a brand manager whose primary job was to help me build the Trent Out Loud brand.

October 21, 2019 -- I posted this on my Instagram:

It's Exclucity's 13th Anniversary. I can't believe I've written 13 of these.

This past year has been a transition year for us and I couldn't be more excited about the future.

As I start my 14th year of business, I just wanna say that I'm ONLY just getting started. EXCLUCITY is just a chapter in my book. I've finally gotten around to dedicating more of my time to my Trent Out Loud platform. Entertainment has always been my first love and I'm finally getting back to it. Hosting, producing, speaking, seminars, and writing my book have all taken a backseat to Exclucity, until now.

STAY TUNED.

. . .

I'm not sure if this is what I should have been posting or if it is what I needed in my life at the time, but it felt good and I went with it.

- **November 13, 2019** -- I bought a brand new 2020 Range Rover Sport HSE with TVs in the headrests, a fridge, and red leather interior. I picked it up at the dealership and filmed the entire process, which I later posted on Instagram.

That Range Rover post is when things started to get really embarrassing for me. I can't even watch that cringy 8-minute video today.

- **November 30, 2019** -- I went to Jamaica for a week and as a challenge I told my Instagram followers that I wasn't going to drink any liquid other than alcohol for seven days. I filmed myself waking up every morning and brushing my teeth with rum, I then posted it.

- **New Year's Eve 2019** -- I hosted a huge party at my house with 100s of people and I posted a video of me singing "I'll Always Love you" on the microphone to a woman that was at the party. My dress shirt was halfway buttoned down, my chest was out and you could see my mother in the background saying, "Trent, put your shirt back on."

- **Jan 23, 2020** -- I went to the Dominican Republic and every night I posted myself drunk doing some dumb shit. I'd wake up every morning with a hangover and the first thing I'd do was to delete all my stories from my phone. I'd get text messages from my friends asking if I was ok and they suggested that I should leave my phone at home or take a break from posting altogether.
I didn't listen.

- **February 2020** -- My schedule was filled with Black History Month events in Toronto so I couldn't take a vacation. I spoke at a Shopify event for Black entrepreneurs, at "My Black Narrative" held at the Soho House, attended The Black Diamond Ball, and I also had my own BHM event at my store that was sponsored by Puma. Each event was filmed and turned into a Trent Out Loud show. I did not go anywhere without a cameraperson and a photographer.

The entire month of February was one major party. I'd post behind the scenes of all these events and, of course, I'd somehow post myself drunk, but then I'd wake up in the morning and delete it.

I felt so good and positive; I was on such a high. I was on the biggest high of my life and was barely sleeping. I was always on the go and no one could slow me down.

I was done stressing over Exclucity and decided to let whatever was going to happen do so. I had my Trent Out Loud platform and I thought I didn't need anything else.

Some may say that I was just trying to lose myself and used dating and partying, etc. as major distractions from trying to save my business. Others looking through a more clinical lens may say my behaviour was a clear sign of bipolar and my not sleeping for days was further proof of the clinical theory.

- **March 10, 2020** -- I spent the night with Tonya and we didn't sleep even for a minute. We were up all night drinking and then I left on an 8am flight to Toronto. I got to my condo, took a power nap and then went out for lunch with another woman that I was dating. She spent the afternoon at my place and left around 6pm. I took another 30-minute power nap, showered and then went out on a date with another woman that I met at a Black History Month event a few weeks before. It was our first time out. We had dinner, then went to a club to drink and afterward came back to my condo. She stayed till about 4am because I was leaving at 5am to catch my 7am flight to Barbados.

  At this point, I hadn't slept in two days.

- **March 12, 2020** -- I landed in Barbados at 1pm, and one of the women that I had met from my last trip there was at the airport to meet me.

  I spent the next four days in Barbados drinking a bottle of rum each day, smoking weed, partying and staying out all night.

  I barely slept while there, making that a total of six nights with practically no sleep.

- **March 16, 2020** -- After my 4-day binge drinking in Barbados, I flew home to Montreal where I stumbled into the house, managed to make my way upstairs to the bathroom and puked green bile for the entire night.

I had alcohol poisoning and thought I was going to die that night.

. . .

I may have been feeling great when I was out partying and having the time of my life but it was all just a fucking lie. That's why I had to do it every night so that the truth and the stress wouldn't sink in. It was pure denial.

I wasn't happy, I was miserable. I wasn't really feeling positive, I was feeling like shit. I was depressed.

I wasn't facing my reality, I was running from it — very dangerously— and running at a pace that my body could no longer keep up with. I'd never been in a place like this before.

But then something happened, something that brought everything I was doing in my life to a screeching halt.

. . .

Covid-19 was on every news channel, the NBA had postponed their season indefinitely, and the world was preparing for a global lockdown.

It was time for me to have a lockdown of my own if I wanted to live to see the end of 2020.

. . .

I'll stop the story right here and pick up on this same night in Book 3, and explain to you...

HOW QUARANTINE SAVED MY LIFE

EXCLUCITY 7 | 2019

Days Away from Bankruptcy

2019

Days Away from Bankruptcy

Back in late 2016, I had an idea of building a new Exclucity concept location called Exclucity 2026. It revolved around the idea of what retail would look like in the future.

This store would be very minimal; cement floors, cement walls, and simple displays for apparel and shoes. It includes futuristic metal sculpture furniture, cool benches, neon lights, giant TV screens and there would be no cash counter because all transactions are done on tablets or smart devices.

The most transcending part of the entire concept was that there wouldn't be any inventory at the actual location. The customer wouldn't be able to try on, purchase or leave with any physical products. There would only be a few displays for the customer to touch and feel but that was it. Customers would have to place their orders on one of our screens, iPad stations, or simply on their own cellphone and it would be delivered to them the next day.

The store would be like physically shopping inside of an online store. Imagine shopping online, but being able to touch and feel the product first, and being able to talk to a live person, and not having to chat online through your keyboard.

My idea was to give the customer an experience rather than a typical retail transactional experience.

There would only be one Exclucity 2026 concept store per major city, as opposed to multiple locations like we're used to now.

Exclucity 2026 was going to be the bridge between new and old school -- the future of retail.

. . .

Fast-forward to *2019* and those plans were a distant memory now. I could no longer think of cool ideas to do in the future, which is the primary role of any CEO. All I could do was think of how I was going to survive the next week, pay my rent and make payroll. That is a crippling feeling for anyone, much less a creative. That's like telling a painter that is used to painting on a 10ft canvas that they can now only paint on an iPad mini.

I felt like I was reduced to nothing.

. . .

When *2019* started, the team and I revisited the idea of opening the Vancouver location -- which I had agreed to delay -- in the hope that a new store there would give us a boost in the arm and a new client base.

Although we had made some minor progress since closing some of our poorly performing stores, sales were still extremely low. On a weekly basis, we were unsure of what would happen next. Since nothing much had really changed after closing the stores and the future looked bleak, I decided that it was too risky to open a new store while we were restructuring.

I phoned my landlord in Vancouver and told him of my horrible financial situation and that I was no longer able to open the location. He graciously let me out of my lease, which does not mean that I didn't lose a tremendous amount of money. I lost my $50,000 deposit but I was able to get out quickly and with no headaches. He was a very cool landlord and that is exactly what we needed at the time.

With the Vancouver location shut down so quickly and out of the way, I turned my attention to Brampton.

My Brampton location was never profitable but it was a really good location. It was located in a mall that gave the Exclucity brand some solid credibility. All the major brands were there, such as Sephora, H&M, Zara, and my favourite store of all time, "The Uniform Boys" (read Book 1 for more details, lol!).

Regardless of what that Brampton location was doing for our brand, it was killing my bank account. I knew that if I wanted a fighting chance at making it, I'd have to close it down. Keisha and I had spent the past six months trying to bring the sales up but nothing was working. That location was just not profitable and we couldn't save it.

In March **2019**, I closed the Brampton location inside the Bramalea City Centre (BCC) mall with the blessing of their management team. I have to give them a shout-out because that could have been a very messy lawsuit but it wasn't.

I called them and explained my situation and they said they would help me out because I was a Canadian entrepreneur. They felt for me and didn't want to make my situation any worse by dragging me through the courts.

How amazing was that? They decided to support me instead of making things a lot worse.

I had to leave the over $300,000 dollars' worth of upgrades that I did so that they could try to sell it off and recoup their losses. I also lost my expensive deposit but all of that is standard and it could have been a lot worse.

I'm very thankful it wasn't.

. . .

As you can see, my **2019** did not start off great, especially from a financial point of view. Not only was I closing stores and losing deposits left, right and centre, but the stores that I managed to keep open weren't performing well either.

The Montreal location was marginally profitable because rent in Quebec is cheaper than in Ontario, but my Queen St. and Yonge St. locations in Downtown Toronto were still losing money.

The sneaker industry was still in a correction and the future was dismal if you weren't part of the Tier Zero crew or a high-end sneaker boutique.

Nike was the clear victor in the Adidas battle but the war wasn't completely over just yet. Yeezy was still lurking around and Jordan Brand was still so focused on burying Kanye that they didn't let up with their onslaught of Tier Zero releases, which continued to make all their regular Jordan releases sit on shelves.

There were so many Jordan Tier Zero releases that sneaker enthusiasts started nicknaming General Retro Jordan releases the "poor man's retros" and nobody wanted to buy them. It was all just a mess. Everything was upside down.

. . .

May 1, 2019 -- I sent this e-mail as an open letter to my friends at Jordan Brand.

E-mail Subject: What message are we sending OUR kids and OUR culture?

This is an open letter to you from me, a dedicated, loyal and trusted Jordan partner of almost 10 years, and this is my opinion of Jordan Tier Zero distribution.

As a businessman, I understand that hard decisions are made for the betterment of the brand. I also understand that not all decisions are always popular and can make some people unhappy.

Since it is impossible to make everyone happy, why not focus on making our core customer happy and let the rest fall in line.

The Jumpman logo has not become one of the most recognized logos of all time because of Paris fashion week, or high-end designers. It was made popular by the hood, the street kids, the Hip Hop Culture and, of course, Micheal Jordan himself. So, I ask you - why are we changing that now? Why have we made the popular Tier Zero Jordan product available only in high-end boutiques? Not all of these boutiques value or respect our culture. Why are we telling OUR kids that these high-end brands are cool? Look what Gucci just did to us after all these years of supporting them. Why are we trying to sit beside high-end brands like Stone Island? Stone Island should want to sit beside us. WE ARE JORDAN BRAND!

Why are we trying to fit in with the European high-end fashion brands? We do not need their approval or sign-off. We don't need them; they need us. We control the cool, not them.

Take next week's Travis Scott release for example. Travis is a HIP HOP artist; how could the upcoming Travis Scott x Jordan release not be available at neighbourhood doors. This is a prime example of a release that should be directed to neighbourhood/street doors that are still connected and serve the community.

Jordan Brand is the first urban luxury street brand for the real street hustlers. Let's bring back our brand full circle and take it back to the 80s where we focused on us.

Thank you for your time.

. . .

I was so nervous to send that email. Lord, I sent it to two or three people at Nike first before sending it off directly just to make sure I wasn't too far off. The feedback was good so I felt confident to send it to Jordan Brand.

The main Jordan executive in Beaverton that I sent the email replied to me positively. He then forwarded it to a few more people and before I knew it my email was forwarded across Nike. It resulted in me getting calls from the Nike Canada leadership team.

I have no idea what kind of immediate or long-term impact the letter had on the Jordan team. All I know is that I was frustrated, upset, and felt let down and left out by a brand that I had helped forge a new path in the Canadian sneaker scene.

Exclucity played a major role in helping Nike Canada change the conversation about sneaker culture in this country and I wanted Jordan Brand to know how I felt.

. . .

Regardless of my frustrations, I knew that things weren't going to change overnight so I continued working on my Trent Out Loud show. I had no money in the bank, the sales at the stores continued to decline and I had no growth plans. My only job at Exclucity was to try **not** to shutdown.

I can't explain to you how depressing that was.

On a daily basis, all I did was balance what little money we had left and try to avoid court cases and debt collectors. I had weekly meetings with my financial team and all we talked about was how I could move money around to make sure that I made payroll and, hopefully, pay off some suppliers.

The one thing that I'm really proud of is that I never missed payroll, not once in my 14 years in business. My first priority when it came to balancing money was the Exclucity staff. Those at the store level did not know that I had money problems, only my upper management team knew. Most of them will be in shock when they read about it in this book.

After the staff and key suppliers, like Nike, were paid, then I'd look to see if there was any money left over for rent. Every month, I'd have to call a different landlord and ask if I could delay my rent cheque for a month or two.

My rent was always behind.

One of my landlords was smart. He amended our lease and agreed to let me only pay him 50% of the total rent, but I had to promise to pay on the first of every month. He said he'd rather get half the rent on time, than all of it months later or maybe no rent at all. It worked; I never missed paying him rent after that.

. . .

Bankruptcy

In *2019*, every meeting with my financial team got more and more depressing. Each week, we ended our call discussing the possibility of bankruptcy and how many days ahead we would have to plan for it, if I had to file, and how we would tell the staff.

All of this shit was so fucking depressing. I don't even know how I managed to bare it weekly.

From around mid-2018 onward, juggling my finances was my main function at the company day in and day out. It was the most disheartening thing you could ever imagine. It was like slamming your car brakes on an icy road. You know you've lost control and you're gonna crash, but you just keep pumping the brakes and turning the steering wheel while looking for the best possible place to crash. It was like living in a nightmare.

I remember telling my accountant that I wish I could just get a job at McDonald's. I'd start my shift at 9am, finish at 5pm, and just go home and not have a care in the world. You can't put a price on a stress-free life.

Try sleeping at night knowing you owe millions of dollars and all you have is a few thousand.

There was always some issue or someone calling me for something. I couldn't even answer my phone anymore unless I knew who was calling. I had so many collectors and unknown numbers calling my phone daily.

I closed three stores in 2018 and two more in *2019* so that I could be more profitable, increase cash flow and try to have a less stressful life but nothing was working. I was still in a losing position, still not profitable.

I was really starting to get fed up and was at the end of my rope. I had exhausted all my options and felt like there was nothing left for me to do but shutdown and call it quits.

Over the past two years of struggling, I had gone to Adidas for help (that was a joke); then I got loans to help me through the downturn (that money only lasted a year or so). I also hired a consultant firm, hired James, went to Nike (they made things worse for me), and eventually hired new employees. I did everything that I could possibly think of but I was still losing money every month. I couldn't take it anymore, but before I decided to throw in the towel I knew I had two options left that I didn't want to look at when all of this started. My back was against the wall so I had no choice.

My last two options were to:

1. Sell Exclucity

Or

2. Remortgage my house, sell off all my personal assets and loan the company the money that it needed to stay afloat while I waited and prayed for the sneaker industry to pick back up.

Every single person on my finance team was opposed to option 2. They made me promise that I wouldn't remortgage my house to put the money back into the business. They were afraid that if I did that and things didn't get better (and there were no signs that things would be), I'd not only lose my company but I'd also lose everything else that I owned and I'd be out on the street with nothing.

Knowing that they were right, I started looking into option 1.

. . .

James and I started shopping Exclucity around to investors at a bargain-basement price, looking for just enough money to cover my debts. We put a deck together with reports, pictures, articles, and anything else that I could find to make the point that Exclucity was a brand worth investing in but our plan didn't work.

It's next to impossible to find an investor when your financial statement showed two years of straight losses and no formula to fix it. You can bring all the pictures and articles that you want to an investor but investors only want to see one thing -- the numbers, and our numbers sucked.

. . .

Option 2

With no other option in sight and being a few Days Away from Bankruptcy, I went behind my team's back and called my bank to take out a personal loan against my house.

What was I thinking? Why would I risk all that?

That's a simple answer for me. At the time, Exclucity was all I had in my life. It's all I had to show my grandmother before she passed away. Exclucity wasn't just a company that generated profits; it was who Trent was, a result of me -- kind of like a child.

I had nothing else; I was alone. I had an empty house that would fill up with people that wanted to party and have a good time, but then they would all leave and I'd be alone. Exclucity was the only thing that gave me purpose. It was the only thing that made me feel needed. Of course, I'd give up my house for Exclucity.

At the time, it was an easy decision to make.

I liquidated all my assets and deposited every penny I had back into the company's bank account. I literally took every single thing I owned and had no money left.

As broken as I was, I was determined not to lose my business.

. . .

I called my financial team and brought everyone together for a special meeting. I thanked them for their hard work and reminded them that we all tried our best over the past two years.

I then told them that I felt the best course of action would be to put together a very conservative and basic plan that I'd manage myself and just hope for the best.

There wasn't anything else James or my financial team could do. We had exhausted all of our options and now that I had invested everything that I owned, I had to be as lean as I could be to stretch things out as long as possible.

It was like putting someone in palliative care.

. . .

The Most Profitable Year Ever

I made this decision in late 2019 before the pandemic hit. I had no idea that in late March 2020, the COVID-19 pandemic would rock the world and as a result I'd be able to make 2020 the most profitable year in Exclucity's 14-year history.

WAIT…. WHAT?????

Yes, you read that correctly, the most profitable year EVER!

Two weeks after the world went into lockdown, I decided to wake the fuck up and take back control of my life and make drastic changes.

A few weeks in lockdown reminded me of who I really was.

I wasn't the guy that was lying down on the bathroom floor drunk in his own puke. That's not who I am. During the lockdown, I was able to connect with myself and I didn't need alcohol or a party to do it. I no longer needed to escape. I was comfortable in my own skin with me. I was able to find the real me again, the guy who sells T-shirt out the truck of his car and builds his own national brands.

That's who the fuck I am!

——————————————————

- In 2020, during a global pandemic, I was able to increase Exclucity's net profits by over 2000%; becoming net profit positive for the first time in over three years and having our most profitable year EVER, in over 14 years.

- I was able to increase Exclucity's gross margin to **over 43% in 2020,** from below 25% in 2018 and 37.5% in 2019.

- At the start of 2020, Exclucity had open lines of credit that were all maxed out. By **March 1,2021, all lines of credit were at ZERO.**

- Exclucity also had outstanding loans owing millions of dollars but by the end of 2020 I brought those loans down to $387K and by March 1, 2021, I paid off all outstanding loans completely and now they are all **CLOSED.**

- In less than one year, I was able to wipe out all of Exclucity's debts completely and I paid myself back every penny I lent the company, and as I write this book **Exclucity doesn't owe a single dollar to a bank, person, or credit card.**

- At the end of June 2021 -- just 6 months into the year -- Exclucity is already more profitable than the entire fiscal year 2020 -- our previous best year -- smashing projections and all of the targets I set.

. . .

I'll tell you exactly how I was able to accomplish everything above in Book 3….

HOW QUARANTINE SAVED MY LIFE

Author: TRENT
Editor: Neil Armstrong
Photographer: NASKADEMINI
Art Director: Marcus Troy
Graphic Designer: AJ Saludo